The
Get Yourself
Organized
Project

The
Get Yourself
Organized
Project

Kathi Lipp

HARVEST HOUSE PUBLISHERS

EUGENE, OREGON

Cover design by Left Coast Design, Portland, Oregon

Cover illustration © Krieg Barrie

Published in association with the literary agency of WordServe Literary Group, Ltd., 10152 S. Knoll Circle, Highlands Ranch, CO 80130

THE GET YOURSELF ORGANIZED PROJECT
Copyright © 2012 by Kathi Lipp
Published by Harvest House Publishers
Eugene, Oregon 97402
www.harvesthousepublishers.com

Library of Congress Cataloging-in-Publication Data
  Lipp, Kathi, 1967-
  The get yourself organized project / Kathi Lipp.
    p. cm.
  ISBN 978-0-7369-4385-7 (pbk.)
  ISBN 978-0-7369-4386-4 (eBook)
  1. Home economics. 2. Time management. I. Title.
  TX145.L57 2012
  640—dc23

                                              2011028814

This book is dedicated to my second-favorite family,

Brian, Lucinda, and Elsa Richerson.

Love you all. Thank you for the love and support for our family.

And Elsa, I promise to never give you

more toys than your mom and dad can organize

(but when it comes to books, I make no promises).

Contents

Acknowledgments 9

Preparing for *The Get Yourself Organized Project*

1. Is This Book for You? 13
2. Eight Basic Rules to Get Yourself Organized 19
3. How the Projects Are Structured 37
4. A Quick-Start Guide 41

Launching *The Get Yourself Organized Project*

The Send-Off 45

Projects for Your Home

Project 1—The Living Room/Family Room 49
Project 2—Bedrooms 57
Project 3—Bathrooms 67
Project 4—Kids' Rooms 79
Project 5—Your Kitchen 91
Project 6—Your Office/Hobby Area 99
Project 7—Garages and Basements 105

Projects for Your Family

Project 8—Your Laundry 113
Project 9—Your Family's Schedule 123
Project 10—Meal Planning 129
Project 11—Grocery Shopping 135
Project 12—Kids' Chores 145
Project 13—Paperwork 149
Project 14—Travel 157

Projects for Your Personal Life

Project 15—Your Schedule 169

Project 16—Getting Out the Door in the Morning 177

Project 17—Your To-Do List 181

Project 18—Your Car 185

Project 19—Your Handbag 193

Project 20—Your Computer 201

Project 21—Your Wardrobe 207

Wrap-Up 215

Dear Reader 217

Acknowledgments

Amanda, Jeremy, Justen, and Kimber—We love seeing you going out into the world and creating homes of your own.

The Dobsons, the Lipps, and the Richersons—Love each and every one of you.

My ministry partners who carry much of this load—Rachelle Gardner, my agent, and Rod Morris, LaRae Weikert, and the entire team at Harvest House Publishers.

Linda Jenkins—Thanks for your fingerprints all over this book.

My team—Lynette Furstenburg, Sunnie Weber, Ginny Chapman, Kimber Hunter, and Bronwyn Swartz—Thanks for using your talents so I can go and use some of mine.

Finally, to Roger—Thanks for being my partner in ministry so I can be your wife at home. Shut the door, baby.

Preparing for
The Get Yourself Organized Project

1

Is This Book for You?

After his 3-month-old son sailed off the roof of his car at 50 mph and landed unhurt in the middle of an interstate highway on Sunday, Michael Murray decided to break the news to his wife gently.

It was, after all, Mother's Day, and Murray, a 27-year-old factory worker, said Monday he did not want to say right out that he had "messed up" by absentmindedly driving off while his son was strapped into a car seat that he had left on the sunroof of his bronze 1987 Hyundai. As her husband sheepishly held Mathew, who was sleeping serenely in white pajamas and sunbonnet, Deanna Murray, 28, recounted the phone call she received from her husband.

"'Come to the emergency room,' he told me."

A surgical nurse, Deanna Murray was on duty at the Medical Center of Central Massachusetts in Worcester when her husband's call came in. The emergency room is down the hall from her work station.

"'Just come down here,' that's all he told me," Deanna Murray said, describing the phone call. "'Mathew has fallen,' he finally said. I ran all the way down the hall."

After learning the full story, Deanna Murray said, "I was in shock. The nurses had to sit me down and hold me. It's a miracle. It really is."

As Michael Murray recounted it, things began innocently enough around noon Sunday when he decided to drive Mathew and his 20-month-old sister to the hospital, where Deanna was working the day shift. He wanted to drop off her Mother's Day gifts—a gold necklace bearing the legend "Number One Mom" and a single rose.

After presenting these gifts, Michael Murray carried his two children back to the indoor garage where he had parked the car. Murray put his daughter into her car seat but then got into the car with Mathew still on the sunroof.

"The garage was dark," Murray said when asked how he could have forgotten about his son.

(Chris Reidy, "Absent-Minded Father Sends Baby Son
Flying Down the Highway," *Boston Globe*, May 12, 1992.)

I first heard this story on a radio broadcast over twenty years ago, and it still gives me the same sick-in-the-pit-of-my-stomach feeling every time I think of it.

But maybe not for the same reason as you.

You see, I think when most people hear or read about the story of young Mathew, their first reaction is, "Thank God that baby is OK." If that is your reaction, congratulations. You are probably a pretty well-balanced, normal person.

However, my first reaction was, "Thank God I haven't done that yet." If that was your first reaction as well, this book is for you.

Here are a few other ways to know whether or not this book is for you:

- if you always know where your car keys are
- if you look at Martha Stewart and think, *Now that's somebody I can hang with*
- if all your dresser drawers slide closed with ease
- if there's nothing in your fridge that's older than your youngest child
- if you think laundry baskets are for folding laundry and not for running around the house gathering up papers, shoes, and fourth-grade science projects

then this book may not be for you. However,

- if you have offered any of your children five dollars if they win the "Where Are Mommy's Keys?" game
- if you have ever entertained someone entirely on your front porch because your house was such a mess
- if your kids automatically know that the hour before Grandma and Grandpa visit is stash-and-dash time
- if you think that getting your shoes on, driving to the ATM, and ordering fast food at a drive-thru is easier than cooking
- if your house is clean and your husband automatically asks, "Who's coming over?"
- if you wear something besides pajamas and slippers to drop off your kids at school, and the drop-off lady asks, "What are you all dressed up for?"

then this book is for you.

You're Not as Disorganized as You Think You Are

I come by my chaos honestly.

I am only one in a long line of people in my family who are disorganized. I have an aunt and uncle who could easily take up a full season on the reality show *Hoarders*, and my dad has stored in his garage non-working electrical parts from the Nixon era. (At least when it comes to my mom's walk-in-closet-sized collection of quilting fabrics, they are organized by color for easy retrieval.)

So when it comes to managing my own household, I was probably a lot closer to being invited to my own clutter intervention than invited to cohost a segment on "Clear Away the Kitchen Clutter" on *Good Morning America*.

Like reading a diet book from someone who has never weighed more than a buck ten, trying to find help from "organizational experts" who have color-coded their laundry hampers since they were three just didn't do it for me.

Out of sheer desperation (and a strong desire to regularly have clean underwear) I would buy the oh-so-magical, super-organization books, start on their perfect systems, and then realize that the author and I had a major communication issue—we weren't speaking the same language. Apparently, my brain was wired completely different than hers was. (Then I would have to organize the book that I was no longer reading into my collection of organizational books.)

The difference seemed to be that while these experts lived to organize, I wanted to get things organized so I could live. I saw organizing as something I wanted to do and then move on. The experts saw organization as the goal in life. (The last time I checked, no one was giving out blue ribbons for the fewest mismatched socks.)

I'm sorry, but I want a little more from life than an improved laundry system.

I bet you do too.

Now don't get me wrong—I have a few friends who love to clean. I mean can't-wait-to-get-down-on-their-hands-and-knees-and-scrub-the-grout-with-a-toothbrush friends. (Come to mention it, I'm wondering again why we're friends.) There again, I realize we have completely different ways of approaching life. While I see the glass as half full, they see the glass as "Are you finished drinking that? If so, go rinse it out and put it in the dishwasher." From these friends and their "kind" I would never be able to learn the art of home management.

I need to learn from people who have the same kind of brain that I do:

- one that loves to get things done—as long as it's quick and easy
- one that doesn't want to waste time on boring or seemingly unproductive things
- one that doesn't want to spend time cleaning a bathroom that's already clean
- one that would rather be watching a good DVD than organizing them on a shelf

When I was describing this book to fellow author Kristin Billerbeck, she looked at me and rolled her eyes. It took only a second for her to confide in me the pain that surrounds her feelings of inadequacy when it comes to organization. "I am so unorganized! My desk is constantly a mess, and I have to color-code everything if I ever want to have a chance of finding anything."

I couldn't believe what I was hearing. While Kristin sees the process—a messy desk, not putting things away when she's done with them—I see the product. Kristin has published more than thirty books and hasn't even reached her forty-fifth birthday. She must be doing something right.

I think too many of us needlessly bag on ourselves when it comes to organization. Kristin has let someone else define organization for her: "The results are not important—the process is." It doesn't matter that we're raising great kids, get dinner on the table every night, and work a full-time job. Since we often can't find our car keys, we consider ourselves a complete and utter failure.

All of us have areas where we already have a system that works for us. So many of us are hyper-organized at work but fall apart when we get home. Some of us enjoy great achievements out in the world, but we feel overwhelmed by trying to meet our family's demands. Some of us are at a place of feeling so buried that we don't even know where to begin.

In this book, we're going to look at the areas that are already working for you and what you are accomplishing. Once you realize that some areas are working, it's only a matter of getting the rest of your life on a system that works for you.

So take heart! You have some struggles, yes. But I would venture to guess you have people in your life whose needs you do meet regularly, a job where you are valued, and people who love you. I bet you meet the needs of many people every single day. Now, I just want to make your life a little easier in the process.

2

Eight Basic Rules
to Get Yourself Organized

I know that eight rules seem like a lot, but as you start to organize this way, I think you'll see how each rule is absolutely necessary. I don't want to tie you down with a bunch of silly rules. I want to give you the freedom of living an organized life and making steps to be who God has created you to be.

Rule 1—Work Backward

I've spent so much of my life living in reaction mode. This real scene is just one example:

> "You need to build a Pentagon out of Popsicle sticks, but it's not due for six weeks? Awesome! I don't have to worry about it for a while."
>
> *Five weeks and six days later...*
>
> "What do you mean you have to have a Popsicle Pentagon by tomorrow? AGGGHHH!"

We all get caught in the occasional crisis. But when you constantly postpone projects and wait until a situation becomes a crisis, that's living in reaction mode. And reaction mode is not a fun way to live.

That's why I want you to work backward. Look at the questions below and think them through.

- What is your busiest day of the week?
- What is your rest day?
- What day does your garbage and recycling get picked up?
- What is your best day to run errands?
- What is the best day to clean house?

Why am I asking you these questions? Because I want you to work backward.

Let's take the question "What is your rest day?" For most people, their rest day (if they have one) is Sunday. So if your goal is to rest on Sunday, think about what needs to happen the rest of the week in order for you to rest that day:

- Your work project needs to be done on Friday so you don't have to stress about it Sunday afternoon.
- You need to marinate something in the fridge on Saturday so you can just pop it in the oven on Sunday.
- You need to run errands on Saturday morning.
- Your kids need to be informed that if they need something for a school project, they need to let you know early in the week and not on Sunday evening.

I've determined that the best day for me to clean my house is Tuesday. (And to be perfectly transparent, since I've been working and traveling full-time, I have someone come in twice a month to do the bathrooms, floors, and kitchen.) But it doesn't matter if I'm the one scrubbing floors or it's someone else, there's a lot I need to do to prepare to clean:

- I make sure that each room is picked up.
- I clean out any stray dishes in the sink so that I can scrub the sink.

- I throw away any food that's past its prime so I can clean the fridge.
- I sweep the kitchen and the bathroom.

Since Tuesday is my cleaning day, I do all those above activities before Tuesday so when it's time to clean, nothing is hampering me.

That's what I mean by working backward. It's making an appointment with myself and then working backward to get it done.

Look at how Nichole Blean, writer and single mom, takes this to the extreme when it comes to scheduling out her days and working backward:

> "This January, I followed in the footsteps of my grandmama, who had particular days for wash, shopping, ironing, etc. I set up Mondays as grocery shopping/cooking days (I cook three meals for my daughter and me, and we eat them through the week), Tuesdays as bill paying/paperwork days, Wednesdays as wash days, Thursdays as tidy up the house days, Fridays and Saturdays I run errands/go to church/do church groups/have fun with friends, and Sundays we have a Sabbath. I work full time and write every day, so this routine helps everything to run smoothly and creates more time for writing.

> "This routine is fantastic in so many ways. I am saving a ton of money on the grocery bill by being more prepared, making meals with what I already have, not wasting leftovers, and using coupons. And I don't really have time for going to the mall anymore since I am streamlining my schedule to open up free time for writing. But the *best* benefit of all is that my daughter (who has lived with my haphazard ways for years) is now getting straight As. I swear it's because of the routine, and she knows what to expect when she gets home from school. Amazing what a little discipline can do!"—Nichole

Rule 2—Apply Pressure Where Needed

When I get a cut on my hand (and I've had plenty of those due to equal parts klutziness and multiple book orders to open), I put a towel on the bleeding area, not on my elbow. I apply the pressure where I need it. So when I devote huge amounts of time and money to purchase and read books on systems of organization, I want them to address my problem, where I'm at, now.

What generally happens, however, is that these books present a plan. And a plan is good, as long as it's a plan that meets your needs. Most of these plans tell me what room to start with or what system to start setting up. Maybe that's fine for some people (those who are good at following a plan, for example), but for me, a better way to roll is to tackle the area that's causing me the most pain and start there. Can you say *garage* anyone?

One of the most stressful things in life is to feel out of sorts, unorganized, and pressured, so it just makes sense to me that you address the most urgent areas first, to get the most relief. As you look over this book, I suggest you start with the areas that are causing you the most stress.

I cover three major life areas in this book: Your Home, Your Family, and Your Personal Life. Each week, I want you to choose a project from each of those areas and apply the pressure where needed.

Now that doesn't mean attack three big hairy projects all at the same time. Let's say that every area of your home feels out of sorts, but your bathroom makes you want to crawl back into bed in the morning. It's complete chaos, you can't find anything, and your collection of vintage hair products could take up a room of their own.

I would say, start with the bathroom.

If your bathroom seems overwhelming, maybe your other two projects for the week are your family schedule and your handbag. Not easy to do, but doable.

However, if your bathroom still feels completely overwhelming, then do just the hair products and save the rest for another week. (Believe me, I have been in bathrooms where the hair stuff could take a week.)

But here's the thing: once you feel some victory in an area that's been causing you pain, you are going to be more motivated to organize the rest of your house, the rest of your family, and the rest of you!

Rule 3—Wait for the Path to Appear

Lieutenant-General Sir John Moore (13 November 1761–16 January 1809) was a British soldier and general known for his military training reforms and innovations. While stationed at Shorncliffe camp (where the barracks are named after him), new buildings were being constructed, and the architect asked him where the paths should go. Moore told the architect to wait some months and see where the men walked, then put the paths there.

What a wise and brilliant man. A man that every woman trying to organize could learn from.

How many times have I set up organizing systems that were doomed to fail because instead of working with my family, the system worked against them? Like the time that I created a cubby space under the desk in the living room for everyone to put their shoes in. The problem? My kids (and their friends) all kick their shoes off as soon as they come in the front door.

So, you might ask, why didn't I put the cubbies by the front door? Because I wanted things to be nice and neat, and I thought it would look terrible to have those cubbies by the front door. What I had instead was a jumble of running shoes and flip-flops by the front door, and some very sad-looking empty cubbies in the living room.

Be kind to your family, and to yourself, and once a path appears, follow the path.

In this book, I may suggest a place to put your keys so you will always find them. If you are in the habit of throwing them on the entryway table as you walk in the door each day, don't let me stop you. You have already created a path.

You may want to put a pretty bowl on the entryway table to hold the keys, but if you've found your path, don't try to create another system to work against you or your family.

As you go through your house and your own life, figure out where the paths have already emerged. Celebrate that you have some patterns in your life, and create systems around those patterns.

Cari Pemberton, a certified family manager coach, gives a great example of waiting for a path to appear: "I recommend setting up a Control Central for that paper pile in your kitchen. Quit spending energy trying to break the habit of opening mail there, and install a trash can or recycling bin (shredder, too, if there is room), plus a file box or other tool for holding bills, school papers, whatever tends to accumulate."

Don't keep fighting your natural habits. Give in and organize around them!

Rule 4—Never Organize Alone

So many of us feel like failures when it comes to organizing because we often start a project but seldom finish. If this is your MO, I'm here to tell you that you are not alone—and you shouldn't organize that way either. *So many of us do better when we have a friend or family member helping us.*

Do you remember the "moving buddy" system in the movie *Toy Story*? The moving buddy system made sure that none of the toys got lost or left behind and that they ended up in the place they were supposed to be.

For the same reasons, I need an organizing buddy. I am fine on my own doing something small like a drawer (that's why, in most cases, you should take it one drawer at a time). But if I'm trying to accomplish something that takes too many steps, I will get distracted, disoriented, and frustrated.

But your friend (or husband or child) can keep you on track, keep you motivated, and keep it fun.

Here are just a couple of examples of how women have used organizing buddies in their lives:

> "My sister Mary came to visit last weekend, and I asked for her
> help organizing the bathroom. I had made bulk purchases of
> soap, shampoo, toothbrushes, and assorted other products
> and had no place to put them, so they'd been on my bathroom
> counter for two months.

"We set up a bunch of laundry baskets and sorted items into baskets labeled 'Cathy's cosmetics,' 'Jim's stuff,' 'Medicines,' 'Travel sizes of stuff we actually use,' or 'Shared stuff' (like toothpaste and toilet paper). Everything else went into the last basket—'Throw out.' In the process, I discovered I had bought the same product more than once because I had no idea I already had it.

"When we were done, I had tossed travel sizes of items I never use, old cosmetics, samples I would never open, old tooth-brushes, hair brushes, etc. And I had room for everything to go under the sink with space to spare. Now there's a drawer for Cathy's stuff, a drawer for Jim's stuff, a center container for shared stuff, and separate shelves for medicines, first aid, and travel. Now it's easy for me to see how many I have of each item.

"Having my sister help was important because there was so much stuff, and not enough room for me to walk to each deposit site. She says she didn't do much, but she was the extra extension to my reach to help distribute into each pile."—Cathy

"For years I sent my daughter Julia to clean her room by her-self to teach her independence, ownership, and responsibility. That didn't work at all for her. She hates being sent to social Siberia to do something she can't stand. After praying about it, I realized that I'm the same way. So lately we work in her room for fifteen minutes, and then she comes downstairs to my room to help me for fifteen minutes. It is so much more fun to have the company.

"I had a friend who suggested we 'project share.' One week we would meet at her house and rearrange the pictures and acces-sories in her three-year-old's room; two weeks later we would meet at my house and paint something. The next time at her house we rearranged her family-room furniture. I loved it because the things that I wanted to be done around my home finally got done. It's great to have someone to bounce ideas off and just to have fun with while I'm completing something that brings joy and order to my world."—Robin

You can see how each of these women (especially young Julia) felt overwhelmed and defeated having to do the projects on their own, but when they had an organizing buddy, it suddenly became freeing (and even fun). Has any verse rung more true than Ecclesiastes 4:9-10?

Two are better than one,
     because they have a good return for their labor:
If either of them falls down,
     one can help the other up.
But pity anyone who falls
     and has no one to help them up.

"They have a good return for their labor"—check.
"If either of them falls down (gets sidetracked, loses interest), one can help the other up"—check.

How to Find an Organizing Buddy

So how do you find an organizing buddy? Here are a couple of ways to find that person.

Give birth to them. Oftentimes, as with Robin and Julia, we fulfill our parents' deepest wish and have a child "just like you." If you both have a problem staying on task, put fifteen minutes on a timer and do your room first, her room next, and chat along the way.

Marry them. When it comes to cleaning the garage, I don't mind the organizing so much. It's the heavy lifting as well as the potential of getting rid of something my husband would miss that make it such a nightmare. Having him help me assures that I don't throw away any electronic stuff that actually is important (plus, he can reach the high shelves).

Offer to help someone else. If you hear of another friend who's struggling, why not set up an arrangement like Robin's: every two weeks, you swap houses and help each other with a project. That means once a month, you are tackling issues you might never have worked on if left to your own devices.

Rule 5—Treat Your Home like a Grown-Up Kindergarten Room

Everything I learned about organizing, I learned in kindergarten.

The most organized rooms most of us will ever experience are at either a school or a hospital. Since I frown on having to go through minor surgery in order to gain organizing tips, I choose instead to draw my inspiration from the classroom.

I have an inside track. My stepdaughter, Amanda Lipp, is an associate teacher at a childcare facility. While she and I were discussing how she wants her room to be set up for her students, I couldn't help but see the similarities between a well-set-up classroom and a well-set-up home.

Here are Amanda's guidelines for a well-run classroom:

1. *Everything has a place and everyone knows where that place is.* Everyone in the house knows where things are because items have an established place. No one has to ask Mom where the tape is because the tape is always in the second drawer of the closet.

2. *Clearly label items with words and a picture.* Label your drawers, bins, tubs, and baskets in a way that everyone in the house can understand. For smaller children, pictures on the labels enable them to help with cleanup responsibilities.

3. *Clearly define each area of the room with boundaries, such as rugs, shelving, or other furniture.* Divide rooms into sections so they are easy to manage, use, and clean up. For example, if your kids have a play area in the corner of your

living room, use a big area rug to define the space so the kids know that every book, toy, and game goes back into the play area clearly defined by the rug.

4. *Keep the room clutter free so children can easily roam and play.* I stay on top of clutter so that we don't have to clear off a table before we eat dinner or move piles of paper from a desk before I can work on it.

5. *Clean up areas when children finish playing and before beginning another activity.* After I'm done with a project, I put it away so that I don't get overwhelmed by the mess.

6. *Arrange each area for maximizing learning capabilities.* The block area has a lot of floor space for building; the reading area has sofas, pillows, and rugs for resting. I look for ways to make my home and the areas in it functional and comfortable.

7. *Arrange the art on the wall neatly, using frames, canvas, backgrounds. A room with too much artwork will feel chaotic and agitating.* I keep things in my home simple and uncluttered. I want the people in my home, not the stuff, to be the focus.

8. *Regularly switch out items for use, allowing the children to experience a wide range of activities while still keeping the areas neat and not overflowing.* Each of our rooms is going to have many different functions, but I will focus on one activity at a time and put away those things I'm not using.

9. *In order for the children to know where items belong, have them help set up the bins and boxes where the items live.* We work as a family to create the systems; we work as a family to keep up the systems.

Even though the saying, "A place for everything and everything in its place," has been around a long time, I still use it in my life today.

The words that make me cringe or even get me downright frustrated are, "Mom (or Honey), where is…?" Even though I have painstakingly gone through my home and labeled plastic drawers and bins to help everyone find things easier, I still hear those irritating words.

However, since I did the work of organizing, labeling, and placing strategically all these bins, it has really made my life easier. Now when I hear those words, "Dear, where is the tape?" I can say, "It's in the closet in my office, in the drawer labeled 'Tape.'" I no longer need to physically stop what I'm doing and find it for them. The tape is in its rightful place.

Rule 6—Begin to Use the Three-Box, Two-Bag System

This is a system you will be using in almost every room in your house, so I want you to gather up everything that you'll need right now:

1. Set up three cardboard boxes, a garbage bag, and a recycle bag, your iPod, and a timer (you can use the one on your cell phone or your oven).

2. Mark one cardboard box "Other Rooms," one "Put Back," and one "Give Away."

3. Give yourself fifteen minutes on your timer and pick a spot to clean out (an area no larger than what you can sort through in fifteen minutes).

4. Go through the area and use the three boxes to sort the contents.

Other Rooms

Anything that doesn't belong in the area you're cleaning goes into the "Other Rooms" box. This includes toys in the kitchen, dog brushes in the living room, report cards in the bathroom, or dishes in the bedroom.

Put Back

This is the box where you put things that belong in the area you're cleaning, but they need to be put back in the right place. If you're straightening up your bedroom, examples of items that you would place in this box are clean clothes on the floor, shoes under your bed, or scarves hanging over a bedroom chair. These all go in the "Put Back" box so once you have your bedroom in order, you just put those items back where they belong.

GIVE AWAY

Clothes your kids have outgrown? Check. Videos your family will never watch again? Check. There is huge freedom in giving stuff away. Here is a great set of criteria for keeping or giving away an item:

- Is it something you or a family member is currently using or wearing?
- Is it something that makes you or a family member happy when they see it?
- Is it something you or a family member will definitely use in the next six months?

If you can answer yes to one or more of those questions, find a home for the item. If not, away it goes.

And a friendly reminder: don't donate garbage. It costs charities time and money to get rid of stuff that you don't want. Don't be that person. Donate only those things that are in decent condition and are worthy of reselling.

GARBAGE BAG

Anything that you don't want and that isn't worthy of being donated or can't be recycled goes in here.

RECYCLE BAG

Recycling regulations vary from city to city, so check with your local municipality or disposal service if you have any question about what should be recycled and what shouldn't.

Once you've cleaned out your chosen area, take the "Other Rooms" box and go around the house putting away all the stuff in that box. Take the "Give Away" box to where you gather stuff to donate or directly to your car to be donated the next time you run errands. Now, since your area is clean and organized, put anything in the "Put Back" box into the spot it's supposed to go.

If this feels totally overwhelming to you, consider having a supportive friend or someone you hire go through these steps for you. There's a lot of freedom in a fresh start.

> "I get caught up in needing the perfect-sized, matching three boxes and bags, deluding myself it will make things easier. This time, I grabbed a flattened box that I reassembled, a wayward plastic container, and I used an old towel to designate a collection area. They were all easy to get, and I wasn't hung up on the logistics of the system."—Tonya

Rule 7—Make a Decision

One of the biggest factors in my home not being as neat as I would like is my fear of making the wrong decision.

- Is that sweatshirt really dirty or can I wear it again? I can't decide, so I throw it over the chair.

- Am I going to have coffee later in the morning? I don't know, so I'll leave the carton of milk on the counter instead of putting it back in the fridge.

- This week my keys will go on the front table in the living room, but next week it seems to make more sense to keep them on the red hutch in the kitchen.

- I never wear that shirt hanging in my closet, but what if it comes back in style? Maybe I'll want it again. Or maybe I'll lose the weight to get back into it. Or maybe I'll find the button that fell off and be able to sew it back on. Et cetera, et cetera.

For some reason, I have a weird hesitation about setting some things in stone. What if it's not the best way to do things? What if someone comes along with a better idea? Perhaps instead of doing laundry, I should go downstairs and defrost something for dinner.

It seems silly that this is a problem for me. I run a business, direct employees, create contracts, and negotiate deals. But when it comes to putting my shoes away, I'm stumped. (Am I going out again tonight or should I put them in the closet?)

So I need to make a decision, set up a pattern, and follow through, even if sometimes it's not the "right" decision. Even if it means taking the four extra steps to get to my keys because at least I'll know where they are.

Here are just a few of those thousands of decisions I now make and follow through on that I didn't make a few years ago. They may seem silly, but they have helped me to keep things picked up and less cluttered in my house.

- My keys, my sunglasses, and my iPod all stay by the front door.
- My purse stays in my room.
- Whenever I put down new food bowls for the cat and dog, I pick up the old ones and put them in the dishwasher.
- I fill up my car anytime I leave the house and it's less than one-third full.
- I run the dishwasher when it's mostly full rather than wait for that one final bowl or glass.
- I have only one book on my nightstand at a time.
- My debit card goes back in my wallet, even if it takes me five more seconds than just throwing it in my purse.
- Worn-once sweatshirts get hung up, even if I'm going to wear them again tomorrow.
- If I'm going to wear the same pj's two nights in a row, I will

fold them and put them under my pillow and not just on the end of the bed.

- If I'm going to watch TV, I will keep laundry going so I can fold while I watch.

- Every time I go downstairs, I first check the second floor for any stray coffee cups or water glasses to take with me.

- When deciding what to do with random papers, I ask, "Will I ever need this again?" and recycle it if possible, instead of, "Now where should I put this paper?"

This final point works for other areas of my life as well. If you're a mom with school-age kids, the amount of paperwork they bring home can be staggering. Try to turn in the permission form and the money due as early as possible. Go through your child's backpack each weekday and dig out any papers due back at school. Fill them out, and put the form and any money due back in the backpack that night. That way it doesn't spend four days cluttering up your counter (and then you have to drive it to school on Friday anyway because it got lost in a pile). The fact that your son doesn't turn it in when he gets to school…well, that's a whole nother book (filled with phrases like "natural consequences" and "staying in the school office while everyone else is on the field trip").

Rule 8—It's Your House, You Make the Rules

Early in our marriage, Roger worked two jobs. He was the worship arts director at our church, and he was also working full-time for a computer company here in Silicon Valley.

Roger had been a single dad for thirteen years. Let's just say between serving at church, raising his kids, and working full-time, the state of his clothes was not the highest thing on his list. Oh, he was always squeaky clean. Pressed? Maybe not so much. So when we got married, I worked hard to make sure that he looked presentable for work.

He kept telling me, "They're engineers. Trust me, nobody cares."

Then one day one of the managers said, "Wow, Roger, you're looking spiffy."

"Yeah, remember?" one of his coworkers yelled out. "He got married."
That was a point of pride for me.

On Sunday mornings, Roger got dressed in the dark because he had to be at church so early. And let's just say that each Sunday there was a fifty-fifty chance how that would turn out.

My thought was, *If he doesn't care about wrinkled shirts around the house, I don't either. But when you leave my house, you're representing me.*

Roger, on the other hand, was less interested in making a fashion statement and more interested in serving at church.

Comfortably crumpled is one thing, but his shirt one particular Sunday looked as if he had rolled it in a ball before putting it on. I spent a lot of that church service not listening to the sermon (sorry, pastor!) and wanting to die. Then I realized, *Nobody cares!* He was there serving God, loving others, and leading his team. I felt like I'd had a spiritual breakthrough.

And then it happened.

After the service, I was hanging by the tech booth, waiting to give Roger a smooch between services, and another church member came up to me, looked me in the eye, and said, "How could you let your husband out of the house looking like that?"

To answer your question, yes, I wanted to die.

After that, I went through Roger's entire closet and vowed that he would never leave the house without looking perfectly pressed. I stepped up his haircut schedule and scrutinized him every time he left the house.

It took me about a month of being a Donna Reed wannabe to come up with the following thought: *Who says something like that?*

Really. Who on earth thinks that any part of that question is OK? I would never in a million years ever dream of saying something remotely so mean-spirited and evil. What on earth was that person hoping to accomplish with that statement?

Yes, now I make sure that Roger's shirts are hung up pressed (or at least passable), but it is the last time I will ever let someone shame me for something as trivial as the condition of a shirt.

There are things that are important to me, to Roger, and to God. Those are the things we need to concentrate on in our home. I let someone else's standards and criticism dictate how I spent my time and my energy.

Also, Roger was probably feeling less like my Hottie Husband and more like a schlump that I was embarrassed to be seen with in public. Not at all how I want my man to feel.

It's your house, your family, your life. You determine what works for you and your family. Roger is fond of saying, "I like a clean house. I love a comfortable home." He doesn't want an uptight wife who will wag a finger if he gets comfy on the couch. He wants to know that there is love and honor in our house (and that it's OK if we occasionally run out of dish soap). Figure out what works for you and your family, not what works for the imaginary church lady hanging out in your head.

I'm not saying that you need to follow the same rules I do; I'm saying figure out what areas of your life are causing you trouble and set up your own rules for that. For instance, if you can never find a pen when you need it at your desk, the rule might be, "All pens when they are done being used go back in the cup on my desk." Yes, even if you might need a pen next to your nightstand one night, don't leave it there "just in case." ("Just in case" is the downfall of those of us who lean toward clutter.)

We all labor under the delusion that we are too busy to take the extra five seconds to put away the milk, put our keys on the hook, or put the mail in the designated spot. The reason we all feel so rushed is that we're spinning around looking for the things we were too busy to put away.

When my friend Tonya read the rule, "My debit card goes back in my wallet, even if it takes me five more seconds than just throwing it in my purse," she had a strong reaction:

> "This is one of those things that when I take the time to do it (yes, literally five seconds), I feel *pressure* to get out of the way for the next customer. Why? It doesn't make sense. We teach our children to take turns. Now I tell myself, *It's my turn*, and

The person behind me can wait. It's not worth losing, even temporarily, my debit card/receipt/keys to give that person a few seconds. In return, when someone ahead of me apologizes for taking a few seconds, I smile and say, 'It's fine. As I tell my kids, we all take turns!'

"Also, now after paying at the store, I pull to an out-of-the-way area to check my receipt. One minute spent doing that saves a trip back (and a failed memory when I do come back) if there's a mistake."—Tonya

Giving yourself permission to take those five extra seconds will reap a host of rewards. You can walk into a store with confidence knowing that your debit card is where it's supposed to be, your sunglasses are safely tucked in their case (and not at the bottom of your bag getting scratched beyond repair), and your keys are in their place so you can find them every time.

3

How the Projects Are Structured

Organizing a room, or even a purse, can be overwhelming if you don't go in with a plan. Below are the five steps I want you to follow for most of the projects you'll tackle as you work through *The Get Yourself Organized Project.* Eventually, these steps will become second nature, and when an area of your life starts to feel out of control, your brain will automatically snap into the Five-Step Plan.

Once you've got your space under control using this plan, I then want you to keep your STEM strong by using your Space, Time, Energy, and Money well. (We'll talk about these more in a moment.) You'll soon see that you're not as rushed, not as stressed, and not as frantic as you were before paying attention to the STEMs in your life.

Understanding the Five-Step Plan

Step 1: Your Plan of Attack

As you approach each of the projects, you're going to need a plan of attack. Make yourself a list of what needs to be done so you can get those lovely check marks we all adore.

Step 2: Sort It Out

For each room you sort, you need to have that set of containers (three boxes, two bags) we talked about earlier when we discussed Rule 6:

Other Rooms. Anything that has wandered into the wrong room is put in this container to be redistributed at the end of the cleanup time.

Put Back. If your shoes are on your bedroom floor, not in your bedroom closet, they go in this box.

Give Away. If your house needs to go on a diet, make sure this box gets filled up regularly. Once it's full, it can be stacked in your garage until someone is ready to go to the thrift store or a local charity.

Garbage and Recycling. I think the use for these two bags is self-explanatory.

Step 3: Clean It Up

Once your stuff is back to its rightful home, it's much easier to clean up without having to stop every thirty seconds to put something away.

Step 4: Label It and Put It Away

In an office, everyone should know where the mail goes, where the pencils are kept, and where to get extra printer paper.

It should be the same for your home. If you asked your kids where the extra toilet paper is kept, would they know? How about incoming mail? Where does it go? If your home feels cluttered all the time, perhaps it's because today you put the magazines in the basket next to your couch, but last week they went on your bookshelves. If you need to label the areas where certain things go until they become a habit for you and your family, do it. A sticky note on your shelf for a month beats clutter for a lifetime.

Step 5: Keep It Up

Give yourself a way to keep up the new systems you put in place. Maybe it's clearing your countertops during the five minutes it takes for your coffee to brew each morning, or setting up a bedtime routine of tidying up your nightstand. Find a ritual that works for you and stick with it. (And I think self-bribery of the chocolate or *People* magazine sort is totally acceptable.)

The Purpose of Organization (It's Not What You Think)

If your purpose in getting organized is to reach the unattainable standards you see on HGTV, you are going to be constantly disappointed (in this book and in your life).

The true gift of organization is getting to live the life that you are designed to live. Being organized is not an end unto itself. It is a way to be able to use your time and talents in the way that God created you.

My favorite flower is the orange gerbera daisy. I just love how incredibly cheerful and optimistic that little flower is. On the gerbera daisy, all the good stuff is at the top—that ridiculously not-of-this-world orange color and the intricate layering of petals that you don't notice until you get right up close. However, I have never heard anyone wax poetic about the stem of a gerbera. It's just not something people think of. But in order for that daisy to bloom and bring me all that joy, it has to have a strong stem.

It's the same with my life. I am created to do a lot of beautiful things—worship my God, love my husband, raise my kids, create a home, work at my job, love on my friends, serve my community, feed my family, and play with my dog. But in order to do those things, I have to have a strong base, a rhythm and order to my life to support everything I want to do. I have to make sure that the stem is strong.

But when your stem isn't strong, that's when things become weaker and out of balance.

Each of us has a limited amount of Space, Time, Energy, and Money (STEM) that we need to balance the rest of our life. When we're depleted in any of those areas, that's when we feel weak, pressed on, out of balance, and not living the kind of life we are created for. So in each of the projects, we're going to make sure that your STEM is strong:

Space. Have you created the space in your life that allows you to do all that you are supposed to be doing? Or do you feel overwhelmed, boxed in, or buried?

Time. Are you wasting time every day in a million little ways? Do you have buffer in your schedule or are you constantly having to compromise because of your lack of time?

Energy. Do you often repeat steps because you aren't organized?

Money. How much money have you wasted because you've bought duplicates of something you can't find?

I want you to live life with a strong STEM. I want you to not feel stretched in any of these areas so that you can be who you are designed to be. So all throughout this book, I will be giving you ways to look at creating more Space, Time, Energy, and Money in your life so that you don't always feel as if you are living on the edge.

Bonus Projects

Throughout the book you will also run across Bonus Projects. These are the cherry on top of the organizational sundae, the little extra things that are a bit of a reward for clearing your space. Maybe it's just putting a bud vase of flowers on a spot you just cleared or getting a pretty basket to put your magazines in. Whatever it is, do something to bless yourself after you've spent the time blessing the rest of your family.

4

A Quick-Start Guide
(I Promise, It's Really Easy!)

1. **Find two friends (at least) to do the project with you.**
   It doesn't matter if they're phone friends, Internet buddies, or face-to-face girlfriends you meet with at Starbucks
   down the street. Location is not important; consistency
   is. Figure out a time to spend together (after everyone has
   read through the book) to come up with a plan for when
   and how you're going to do the projects.

2. **Pick a room—any room.** I would pick the room that's
   giving you the most stress and start there. You'll feel better
   when some of the pressure is taken off.

3. **Print out *The Get Yourself Organized* cards.** Go to our
   website (www.ProjectsForYourSoul.com) and print out
   the cards for an easy reference for each room. It will be
   much handier than referring to the book for each step of
   the way.

4. **Decide on a start date.** It can be tomorrow or two weeks
   from now. Mark it in a big bold way on your kitchen calendar. Set up reminders on your computer. I definitely recommend that you give yourself a couple of days to get ramped
   up and pull together a plan that you're excited about.

5. **Come up with your plan.** *You* decide what steps you're going to take each day. I've provided a variety of ideas, but it's up to you to decide how you'll carry out each day's project.

6. **Share your project plan** with your accountability partners. I recommend that you make copies of your calendar to share with your accountability partners. There is a Project Planning Calendar available on our website for you to print out and use. That way, you can commit to pray for each other, as well as lend support on days that may be particularly challenging. Who knows, your accountability partners may have some great, creative ideas to share.

7. **Be flexible.** If one of the projects doesn't line up with your life, swap it for another day. If you are going on vacation for a couple of days, then postpone your current project until you get back. The intention of *The Get Yourself Organized Project* is not to add stress, but to make your life simpler by removing the clutter from your life and helping you stay organized. Just do something, intentionally, every day.

8. If you're doing this as a group, be sure to **check out all the free group resources** on our website (www.ProjectsFor YourSoul.com). There are lots of great tools, forms, and other fun stuff to make this a great group project.

Launching
*The Get Yourself
Organized Project*

The Send-Off

Congratulations! I am very excited that you have made a commitment to live with less chaos and more peace in your life.

There are going to be some days when *The Get Yourself Organized Project* is going to be hard to complete. It would just feel easier to close your bedroom door than to spend any time organizing it. And your kids' rooms? You may be feeling like it would be easier to just move and start all over.

My prayer is that you don't become discouraged. You deserve to live in a house where you can find your keys every day. You need some peace.

My prayer for you is that when you or anyone you love comes home, they find it a soft place to land.

Kathi

Projects for
Your Home

Project 1

The Living Room/Family Room

A good place to start your project to get organized is to tidy up your living room or family room, or focus on one area of that room if you're overwhelmed by the thought of doing the whole thing.

Step 1: Your Plan of Attack

Just like the TV that's housed there, the living room/family room has undergone an evolution over the past few decades. If you've watched old *Leave It to Beaver* reruns, you would think that the living room is only for the family to gather around the TV and for polite chitchat with company.

My living room has served a variety of functions over the years:

- Kids' computer room
- Home business office
- Playroom
- Home-school classroom
- Bible study meeting room
- Movie theater
- Temporary bedroom (for kids between dorm move outs and apartment rentals)
- Guest room
- Game room
- Library

The first thing you need to do is be honest about what your room is used for. Is it a playroom for your kids? An art studio? Homework central? Take a few minutes and write down all the different activities that happen in your living room/family room. Don't be influenced by what your neighbor's living room is used for or what your house growing up looked like. This is about you, your family, and your needs. Remember Rule 8: "It's Your House, You Make the Rules."

Activities that happen in your living room/family room:

Make sure that the furniture in your room is meeting the needs of how you use the room, not how you think other people think a living room should look. When Roger and I got married and combined our households (with two teens each), we lusted over the idea of a large house to contain our growing brood. After looking at different options (and our bank accounts), it didn't make sense to go into extreme debt to buy a bigger house for the couple of years we had three out of four kids living there. That meant I needed to give up the fantasy of having a *Country Living* kind of living room and let the room meet the needs of our family at the time.

People would chuckle as they walked across the threshold of our house, greeted by the backs of three kids on their computers lined up along the back wall of that living room. While I hated how it looked, we always had our kids where we could see what was going on computer-wise, and it was just a phase. (OK, the living room is now used—in part—to run our home business. It looks a lot snazzier than when I had all those teens in there.)

When you get real about the stage you're in, that's when you can stop fighting with your living room. Create the room that you need now and keep a file of all those white couches you want for when the kids move out.

Divide and Conquer

If tackling the whole room seems overwhelming, start by dividing the room into areas or activities that happen in the room and tackle just one area for this project. (Don't worry, you're going to stay on top of this for the rest of your life. You'll have plenty of time to hit all those other areas.)

Here are some smaller areas that you could attack for this project:

- Videos
- TV area/gaming systems
- Bookshelves
- Game area
- Play area
- Reading area

If your living room/family room doesn't seem that overwhelming, then you can do the whole room in one project.

Grab your three boxes (from the Three-Box, Two-Bag System I described earlier in "Eight Basic Rules to Get Yourself Organized") and start going through everything in your living room that is out of place.

Step 2: Sort It Out

OTHER ROOMS

Anything that belongs in another room is put in this box. It's so easy for things to be dumped in the living room and never make it back to their original owner. For years in our house, we had a permanent "Other Rooms" basket in our living room. Our kids were real kids who left real stuff around. I would throw stray shoes, books, etc. into the basket. When it started to overflow, I had one of the kids redistribute all the "lost soles" back to their owners.

PUT BACK

If things belong in the living room but have just wandered from their original home, this is the box where they need to go. We will get back to this box soon.

GIVE AWAY

I think you'll find the "Give Away" box especially useful when it comes to DVDs you no longer watch. (In other words, don't save that copy of *Thomas the Tank Engine* for your grandkids when your kids are in junior high.)

Again, analyze what your room's real function is. If that thing in your hand no longer meets your or your family's need, give it to a family that can benefit from it.

Step 3: Clean It Up

Time to give the room a quick cleaning (this is not the time to start reupholstering the couches).

Go through the room and give any electronic equipment a good dusting and clean the screens. Be sure to check the owner's manual for cleaning your TV and computer screens as these can be damaged if you use regular cleaning products.

Shake out area rugs, vacuum the carpet or floor, and give the windowsills a once-over.

My method for cleaning windowsills is to go over them with a rag and some cleaner once or twice a month. But once a year, when they're looking dingy, I just repaint them—only the windowsills, but it freshens up the whole room. I do this with our painted-stairs banister that starts to look worn about every six months.

Step 4: Label It and Put It Away

No, I don't mean create a labeling system for your DVDs so they're cross-referenced by leading man and genre. What I do mean is to establish an area for your different activities—a shelf for DVDs, a shelf for

CDs, storage for your Wii system, and a place to put your books if this is where you read.

If you're frustrated by all the magazines that pile up in your living room, get a basket that is now "The Magazine Basket" for them to land in. If your daughter's art supplies always end up in the living room (and you're OK with her working in that space), find a pretty basket that she can store them in at the end of her creative time so you aren't always tripping over crayons and markers.

Make sure that your daughter knows where the basket goes at the end of the day. How is she supposed to put something away if there's never been a spot designated for it?

Step 5: Keep It Up

Keep looking for ways to control the clutter that sneaks back in.

One of the best investments we ever made was a TV stand with storage underneath it. This is where the Wii and PlayStation are stored. I force our kids to go through it whenever the drawers have trouble closing. Most of the time, it's all hidden and I never have to worry about it unless I want to use Wii Fit. (And really, how often is that?)

Keeping the STEM Strong

Space

DVDs. One of the areas that got out of hand for us was our video collection. We had so many videos that were given to us for Christmas or birthdays that it was getting out of control. If you face a similar issue, here are a couple of ways to deal with it:

- Roger's brother Randy and his wife, Debbie, have taken all their DVDs out of their cases and put them in a huge binder with pages designed to hold DVDs/CDs. This solution is only for people who are already somewhat organized and will take the time to put the DVDs back when they're done. Debbie is one of those naturally organized people (in a good, cool way).

- Get rid of a bunch of DVDs. I know that's hard to read, but if staying organized is a priority, the less you have to organize, the better. Roger and I still have a decent-sized DVD collection, but we go through it regularly and get rid of the ones we won't watch again. A fun way to do that is to post the title on Facebook, and whoever responds first gets the DVD. It costs less than two dollars to mail a DVD, and how great will it be to make someone's day by sending them a DVD in the mail. If you're in a financial place where two dollars is too much, you can always just limit your giveaway to friends who are local.

Time

Remotes. Ugh. How many days of my life have been wasted looking for remotes? A big basket on the coffee table can eliminate the hide-and-seek as long as everyone in the house knows where it goes. And make it a big basket so teens don't have to work too hard to put the remotes away.

Don't let it get messed up in the first place. Limiting the food that is eaten outside the kitchen/dining room is a huge time-saver when it comes to your living-room carpet. I have no problem saying that adults are allowed to have drinks in the living room, but kids can't. Each of our kids has had to earn the right to have food in the living room by cleaning up after themselves and busing their own dishes.

Energy

Quick pickups. Commercials are a great time to keep up on your living-room pickups. I know you can blast through all the annoying car ads now thanks to DVRs, but instead of hitting fast-forward, go ahead and use those minutes to fold blankets, put your kids' stray shoes in a basket, and neaten up your magazines.

Baskets. If your living room, like ours, tends to be one of the busier rooms in the house, you may want to have a basket in that room for each member of the family. It's a quick way to clean the room and will save you a lot of stress when you want to quick clean.

Money

Cable. Look at the cable channels you're paying for. Do you really need everything you're auto billed for each month?

Library. We got into the bad habit of not using our public library for books. Finally, when we returned, I was surprised to discover the DVDs that were available. Between the new authors I discovered and several BBC series that I'm now addicted to, all free, the library is the best deal on the planet. The key for us was having a bag by the front door to store all those books and DVDs that need to be returned.

"To make this easier on myself," my friend Jennifer says, "a few years back I bought a canvas reusable tote from our local library. It has a nice picture of our library on the front. It's our library bag and the library books, CDs, and DVDs live in it until they are returned. I can't help but be reminded of its use when I see it."

However, not every family should use the library or use it all the time. Some of us (and I can definitely be this way at the busier times of my life) have the best of intentions and check out a dozen books to read or DVDs to watch, and they sit by the front door, racking up late fees. I limit my library use to the summer when I have the luxury of time to catch up on all those books I've missed during the rest of the year.

If you've tried the library on several occasions and it doesn't work for your family, don't stress about it. You are not a bad person if you have problems getting the materials back on time. But don't set yourself up for failure either.

Bonus Projects

I firmly believe that every woman should have one spot (besides her side of the bed) that is fully her own. My goal is to have a chair that is all mine in the living room. Until then, I have a spot on the couch that has a place for a drink, my magazines, and a comfy quilt for when the California airs dip into the mid-60s.

My friend Shannon talks about her special spot:

> "I love your placing value on a woman having a place of her own. When you mentioned desiring to have your special chair, I thought of my sofa. Our 'grown-up living room' is my space. It's where I write and where I sit on my big, crazy yellow sofa we found for a song at an antique market downtown. It makes me smile. We've repainted the entire downstairs of our home just to flatter this crazy sofa. It's amazing how that one special piece of furniture can really lift a girl's spirits."

Create a spot that you can call your own for a quiet sit-down, a coffee, and some peace.

Project Reports

> "The living room didn't seem overwhelming, and I thought it wouldn't take me too long, armed with my boxes and bags. The overall project, for the most part, took about three-and-a-half hours. And this could have been better utilized time had I not had my six-year-old, six-month-old, and husband lurking around. My advice—get them out of the house or hire a babysitter. Every request for juice, diaper that needed changing, snack, or conversation led me down a path away from my project.

> "In the end I had three paper bags of garbage, two extra large plastic bins of donated items, and two IKEA shopping bags full of stuff to put away. The IKEA bags were perfect for this project—only ninety-nine cents and larger and stronger than paper or plastic bags, but the soft sides made it ideal for holding lots of items."—Jennifer

Project 2

Bedrooms

You not only need a good night's sleep, you deserve a good night's sleep.

This is a special challenge in our home. Roger has had problems sleeping for as long as we've been married, and reportedly for a dozen years before that. Our bedroom resembles the Stanford Sleep Clinic with blackout shades, a sound machine, and a mattress that cost us more than my first car. The problem is this is also my office. I need to keep the majority of my writing-related stuff in this room. If I'm not vigilant, the stuff can take over, and our room stops being a relaxing retreat and starts resembling an overworked air traffic controller's desk.

Your bedroom should be a safe place for you (and your husband, if you have one) to land at the end of the day. The only way to do that is to get honest about the use of the room. If you keep pretending that you don't really work in there, you'll never have a place for your work, hobby, or exercise-related stuff and it will continue to pile up on your dresser, your floor, and any other flat surface in that room.

Step 1: Your Plan of Attack

Let's keep it simple for now. I want you to attack your bedroom except for the clothes. Don't work on your dressers, closets, or trunks. (Don't worry, we'll get to that in Project 21.) For now, let's deal with the rest of your bedroom.

How do you use your bedroom? You have to be honest in your answer here. So many women think all they use their room for is resting, relaxing, retreating, and romancing. They have this fantasy bedroom in their minds, while in reality, this is where you fold the laundry, stash unwanted stuff, and do some work.

Spend a moment and write in the space below all the activities that really happen in your bedroom. Here are some suggestions to get you thinking:

Sleeping	Exercising
Working	Reading
Folding clothes	Computer time
Sex	Family time
Quiet time	Talking

My goal is to have my bedroom be only a retreat for Roger and me. Yes, I have my office in there, but sometimes (as when you have a small house) you have to make unwanted choices. That's why, even though I would love to have my own office, we compromise. I do my best to have a hard stop from work at 7:00 each night. I spend a little time cleaning up my area, creating a To-Do List for tomorrow, and shutting down.

We even installed cabinets in the bedroom (the wall-mounted kind above the desk) to store all of my work stuff. Yes, it looks like an office, but it looks like a clean office and isn't a distraction when it comes to couple time.

If you've determined that your bedroom needs to be multifunctional, go in with a plan to make it really function. So what if, for a while, your nightstand is a filing cabinet. Make it the prettiest, most romantic filing cabinet you can find (or cover it with a pretty cloth).

The goal is to acknowledge what you use the room for, and then have only those items in there. In other words, if part of your bedroom is an office, make it a clean, functioning office. However, if you have school projects or an unused stationary bike, get them out of there.

AREAS

Once you've determined what your bedroom is being used for, start sectioning off your room. If you work in the bedroom, then create a work area. Don't let your work stuff stray all over the room. Conversely, don't put your folded clothes (that you haven't gotten around to putting away) on your work desk.

Even when I had my postage-stamp-sized, one-room apartment in Japan, which was smaller than the bedroom I share with Roger now, I had sections. Yes, they were tiny sections (my entire kitchen was the size of a single bed), and some areas were multifunctional out of necessity (I stored my futon during the day so I could bring out my sit-on-the-floor dining table). But every area had a purpose, and I could name each area and what purpose it served. Remember Rule 5, "Treat Your Home like a Grown-Up Kindergarten Room."

Go ahead and list the *areas* of your bedroom here:

Now that you have *areas* in your bedroom, anything that doesn't belong in one of those areas needs to find a new home (or be given away).

Never forget the main purpose of the room is sleep, rest, and connecting, making it as distraction free as possible. If areas of your bedroom are making it hard to rest (the computer beckons you, you trip over your stationary bike every night on the way to the bathroom), those areas need to find another place outside your room.

Step 2: Sort It Out

Time to grab your three boxes and two bags (you're getting the hang of this system by now, right?). Make sure you go everywhere in your bedroom—look especially under the bed! It's amazing what can hide out there.

OTHER ROOMS

If you have things besides clothes lingering in your closet, such as sports equipment or memorabilia, now is the time to deal with those. We'll come back to the bedroom another time to organize your clothes (Project 21). I don't want to overwhelm you with too much right now and find you in a puddle on your closet floor.

You've probably used your room as a dumping ground when guests come over. It's time to put all those stash-and-dash items back in their real homes. I also know that a lot of kids' stuff can make it into your bedroom if you're not careful.

Part of the reason I love staying in hotels is the clutter-free environment they offer (at least until I unpack). Sadly, our bedroom, left to its own magnetic devices, will collect all the picture frames, candles, lotions, books, magazines, and tchotchkes that make it past the front door. If I'm not careful, our room can resemble an excavation site on *American Pickers*.

It sneaks up on me. I hadn't realized that I had let a scented-candle store take over my boudoir. We had fourteen candles in our room. Now I like a good-scented candle as much as the next girl, and often receive them for gifts. But fourteen? Was I planning on going off the grid and abandoning electricity? No. I realized it was perhaps time to get my candle supply down to an even half dozen.

Keep what you use in your bedroom, but get rid of (or store, in the case of candles or other things you know you'll use) anything that you have multiples of that you are not using.

As you go through your room, consider what it would take for you to have that sense of peace you'd have entering a clean hotel room. I'm not saying you should try to live up to the impossible standard of a large corporation that daily employs a team of maids. However, when you consider keeping your collection of frog figurines on your night-stand, think about the feeling you want to achieve as you enter your room.

PUT BACK

Save this box for after you clean.

GIVE AWAY

If you aren't using it, are never going to use it, it doesn't bring you joy when you see it, give it away. It might even be a candle, but you don't like the smell, or a picture that you love, but you hate the frame. You can always put the picture in a new frame.

I knew I should get rid of a set of sheets that I paid way too much for because Roger doesn't like the feel of them. I kept hanging on to them, knowing I would never use them, but I just hated giving away that much money.

Finally, Roger couldn't take it anymore. "You know I never want to sleep on those sheets, right?" he asked.

"I know. But they were so expensive."

"So are you saving them for when I die?"

I donated the sheets to Goodwill the next day.

GARBAGE AND RECYCLING

Don't let your room become a dumping ground. Get rid of all those pieces of mail and other papers that are cluttering up your room. Recycle magazines you're no longer reading and don't let them pile up. When you start to consider creating a nightstand out of all your saved-up issues of *Real Simple*, just understand that you have a problem.

If any of your throw pillows or area rugs are looking a little tired, it might be time to retire or recycle them.

Step 3: Clean It Up

Now that you've decluttered, it's time to give your room a good cleaning. Not a deep cleaning—that can be for another day. Just do a few things to make it a little bit brighter and a little bit better:

- Wash your sheets and flip or turn your mattress. Around three times a year we do this: we flip in the fall and spin (turn) in the spring and on Daylight Savings day.
- Dust the room
- Clean your mirror
- Vacuum

Step 4: Label It and Put It Away

Now that you've determined what stays and what goes, it's time to put it all away. Here are some of the storage/living tips I use in the bedroom.

UNDER THE BED

I know that some organizing gurus will tell you to keep under your bed completely free of any storage. That would be lovely if I lived on a sprawling estate à la Mr. Darcy's home in *Pride and Prejudice*. Alas, I live in a condo in San Jose, California, and every square inch of usable and accessible space must be utilized. My friend Tonya says, "Bed risers and plastic storage tubs are great for under-the-bed storage, but only for what fits around the perimeter of the bed." Yep, if you need to wait for your sixteen-year-old basketball player to get home to reach the beach towels stored under your bed, your system is going to fall apart.

Make sure to label each clear storage unit well so you can see it when bending down to peer under your bed. Remember Rule 5: "Treat Your Home like a Grown-Up Kindergarten Room." If you can't easily identify what's in each storage tub and where it belongs, you have too many tubs under your bed.

Step 5: Keep It Up

The key is to not let anything into your bedroom that isn't supposed to be there. That, along with a couple of daily rituals, will make your room easy to keep up.

Make your bed every day. No, my sheets aren't perfect under the comforter, but if my standard were perfection, I would never make the bed. By pulling up the comforter and placing the girly pillows back on the king-sized bed, half the bedroom is clean and in order.

Bus every day. Just as tables at a restaurant need to be bused, sometimes so do other areas of our house. Roger and I both like water bottles in the bedroom in the summer, and I like a cup of decaf coffee or tea before bed in the winter. Roger likes fat-free popcorn before his head hits the pillow. If we aren't diligent, we could have a full load of dishes hanging out upstairs.

Keeping the STEM Strong

Space

> "Try to get rid of any flat surfaces that will become a place to put stuff, which then becomes pile stuff. If you have a dresser, place picture frames, a jewelry box, or other items on top of it to discourage the buildup of stuff."—Christy

Time

Sheets. The number one way to save time folding sheets is to not do it. Strip your sheets and put them immediately into the washer, dryer, and then back on the bed. I am so willing to have an unmade bed for a couple of hours if it means not wrestling with sheets.

I could not agree more with the declarative title of author Lisa Quinn's book on organizing, *Life's Too Short to Fold Fitted Sheets.* Yes, I do fold my fitted sheets. But not in a twenty-step process that any organizing guru would approve. I just turn them upside down, folding them corner to corner with the hangover part of the sheet in the middle of the fold. No, they don't lie flat, but since I'm storing only one set in a lidless tub under our bed while the other set is on the bed, I don't mind that it's taking up a bit of extra room.

I store the winter sheets (flannel) in with my winter clothes, making it easy to pull everything out at once.

If you find sheet storage frustrating, maybe you just have too many sheets. Pull out your favorite two sets for summer, your two favorites for winter, and donate the rest. Think of all the room you'll save if you aren't storing enough linens to operate your own bed-and-breakfast.

In our house, everyone's linens are stored in their rooms, under their beds, making the changing of the sheets for each room easy.

> "Here's a gem I use for sheet sets: After you fold them, put the sheets in one of the pillowcases. When you need to grab a set, it will all be right there."—Karin

Energy

How many pillows do you have on your bed? Or should I say, how many pillows do you have on the floor of your bedroom that, in your fantasy, should be on your bed? Getting more pillows isn't going to make you want to make your bed more. Once you get in the habit of making your bed every day, then you can add the extra pillows that make it look great.

Money

We have a washable coverlet (think quilt-like blanket) that goes over our comforter (that costs a *ton* to clean) for everyday wear. That way when you have a kid, a dog, or a spouse that maybe isn't super-careful about keeping it clean, you can just throw the coverlet in the washing machine and dryer, making trips to the dry cleaner less necessary.

Bonus Projects

Roger is amazing when it comes to bringing home flowers for special occasions. (I keep telling him he needs to do webinars for husbands.) I get a week or so of enjoyment in my kitchen or living room from those. Recently, after a few days away, I came home and my daughter had placed a rose from our garden in a tiny bud vase on my desk in our bedroom. I don't know why that had never occurred to me before, but having that sweet rose in our bedroom to greet me in the morning and to catch a whiff of as I was falling asleep brings me joy.

What is something that doesn't cost anything that you can do to pretty up your room? Maybe you can grab some lavender from your garden and put it in a bud vase on your nightstand. Maybe it's reframing a picture of your husband to put on your nightstand. (Or maybe it's reframing a picture of the other love of your life, your dog.)

Project 3

Bathrooms

I have given up on having an adorable bathroom.

I have been in hundreds of houses over my lifetime, and I have the smallest bathroom I have ever seen. Even my kids' bathroom is bigger than ours. I have gone from wanting a luxurious bathroom to one that is clean and can help get me ready in the morning as quickly and hassle free as possible.

So once I got over the *Extreme Home Makeover* fantasy bathroom, where there's a sink for every person and animal in the house (as well as enough room to hold a Pee Wee football game on the hand-cut Italian marble floor), I got down to the business of making it fun, functional, and a little bit quirky.

Step 1: Your Plan of Attack

Figure out ahead of time where the storage places are in your bathroom. If you have a tiny room like mine, you may need to think outside the medicine cabinet. You probably won't be able to do all these storage ideas right away, but if you struggle for space, you'll want to figure out a long-term plan.

Shoe bags. They aren't just for shoes anymore. I have a clear shoe bag that is mounted to the wall behind my bathroom door. Two rows of the shoe holder house my makeup. Then two rows hold all my hair products, combs, and clips. Other pockets hold a variety of other items I need daily or not-so-daily, such as sunscreen, cotton swabs, and facial cleanser. The clear bag makes it easy to find these as quickly as possible.

If you're using this idea in your kids' bathroom, you could label each of the holders with the product category or your kids' names. I'm not saying they'll automatically put their hair gel back, but when it's time to pick up the bathroom, it will be a lot simpler. My friend Robin has a different use for her shoe organizer:

> "I store all of my girls' hair bows and barrettes in the shoe-organizer pockets, organized by color. All of the red hair bows, ties, etc. go in one pocket. Makes it easy for them to figure out what matches and keeps the counter cleaned off."

Extra shelves. Just because our bathroom didn't come with shelves doesn't mean I can't have them. Roger and I went to IKEA and got one set of open shelves for our bottles (perfumes, shower gels, lotions, etc.) and one set of small shelves with a door that serves as our medicine chest. Toothpaste, deodorants, and medicines that aren't affected by the humidity all belong here.

And even if you can't get any of these storage options just yet, hopefully you'll be getting rid of enough stuff that it won't matter quite as much.

Step 2: Sort It Out

Grab your three boxes and two bags and let's get started.

OTHER ROOMS

Anything that has migrated to the bathroom that doesn't belong there needs to go home.

If you buy in bulk but have a tiny bathroom, perhaps it's time to find a different place to store those five other deodorants, seven extra toothbrushes, or the gallon-sized container of shampoo your husband insists on getting because "Shampoos are all alike, right?"

If you currently keep medicines in the bathroom, you may want to think about changing locations. The humidity of the shower can cause meds to stick together over time. A hall closet (with a safety lock for little kids) is ideal.

Again, if the space is small, everything needs to earn the right to be in the bathroom. If it hasn't earned the right, it either needs to find a new home or be tossed.

PUT BACK

Hold on to this box until it's time to put everything back.

GIVE AWAY

While you won't be donating your used-only-once straightening gel to Goodwill, my friend Melissa told me about a "product swap" she and some friends had:

> "One day my friend Trish and I were talking about all the bath and body products we had sitting around that we never used. Trish emailed a couple of our friends and we decided to have a product swap. We all went through our makeup, hair products, lotions, skin care, nail polishes, and shower gels and brought whatever we weren't using to swap. The fun part was that we got to try on blushes, sample perfumes, and had a grown-up slumber party (without the slumber). Each of us went home with about the same number of items we came with and had a great time in the process."

While I would discourage swapping mascara, I love the idea of swapping all those products and getting stuff you'll actually use.

If you use your bathroom to store your towels, go through the ones you actually use and get rid of the rest. Old washcloths can be used for cleaning, and towels can be dropped off at most animal rescues for bedding. (Check with the shelter first, of course.)

GARBAGE AND RECYCLING

Reading material. I am guilty of keeping too many magazines, catalogs, and other fun stuff in our tiny bath. I have a policy that if a magazine is over a month old, I need to go through it, rip out the articles I want to keep, and recycle the rest.

Cosmetics and products. Other items to toss or recycle include the shampoo that makes your hair frizzy and the blue eye shadow that you kept from junior high. In fact, here's a list from a cosmetician on when to get rid of makeup that's been hanging around:

- *Lipstick*—get rid of it if it changes smell or consistency
- *Eyeliner, mascara, eye shadow*—three to six months (any longer and it breeds bacteria and could cause eye infections)
- *Blush*—one year
- *Foundation*—one year (sooner if it has a strange odor)
- *Pressed powder*—six months to one year

I want you to stay healthy and sty-free. Do us both a favor and get rid of anything that has the potential to blind you.

And I love the idea this cosmetician gave to make sure you always know how long to keep that Maybelline: "When you first buy a product, take a permanent marker and write the date on it. You'll know at a glance when it's time to replace."

I wear very little makeup day to day, but I want good stuff for when I'm speaking or going out with Roger. I invest in those items that have a longer shelf life (lipstick, blush) and spend less on those things I want to change more frequently (pretty much anything to do with the eyes). I don't care how much it costs; no mascara is worth an eye infection.

Samples, giveaways, and travel-sized stuff. I have an addiction to travel-sized products. Some are from places I've stayed in my travels for my job, but some are just travel-sized items that I've purchased from Target. The problem is, apparently, if I don't go through my stuff regularly, I just assume that I must be out of something and pick it up the next time I'm at the store.

To address that problem, I created a see-through bin under my sink, and just this week, when I needed to pack for a trip, I went shopping in my "travel bin" and found the shower gel and dental floss I needed (in handy, travel-sized containers). If you're like me, an "out of sight, out of mind" kinda girl, make sure you store your extras in a clear see-through box so you know what's there. I also limit my supply to two of each item.

In addition to my travel bin, I keep a small funnel in my bathroom that has helped greatly in refilling some of my travel-sized containers with all those gels and hair products that I take on trips.

GUIDELINES FOR DRUG DISPOSAL

I used to hold on to medicines too long because I wasn't sure how to safely get rid of them. Here is what the Health and Human Services website says to do about all those meds, prescription and otherwise:

- Follow any specific disposal instructions on the drug label or patient information that accompanies the medication. Do not flush prescription drugs down the toilet unless this information specifically instructs you to do so.

- Take advantage of community drug take-back programs that allow you to bring unused drugs to a central location for proper disposal. Call your household trash and recycling service to see if a take-back program is available in your community. The Drug Enforcement Administration, working with state and local law enforcement agencies, sponsors National Prescription Drug Take-Back Days throughout the United States.

- If no instructions are given on the drug label and no take-back program is available in your area, throw the drugs in the household trash, but first take them out of their original containers and mix them with an undesirable substance, such as used coffee grounds or kitty litter. The medication will be less appealing to children and pets, and unrecognizable to people who may intentionally go through your trash.

- Put them in a sealable bag, empty can, or other container to prevent the medication from leaking or breaking out of a garbage bag.

FDA's deputy director of the Office of Compliance, Ilisa Bernstein, offers some additional tips:

- Before throwing out a medicine container, scratch out all identifying information on the prescription label to make it unreadable. This will help protect your identity and the privacy of your personal health information.

- Do not give medications to friends. Doctors prescribe drugs based on a person's specific symptoms and medical history. A drug that works for you could be dangerous for someone else.

- When in doubt about proper disposal, talk to your pharmacist.

Bernstein says the same disposal methods for prescription drugs apply to over-the-counter drugs as well.

Step 3: Clean It Up

Do a quick cleanup of your bathroom. This is not the time to get bogged down in scrubbing around the tub with a toothbrush. I just want you to clean those areas (under the sink, shelves, and so on) that are often ignored, and do a basic cleaning of the rest of the room. But as long as you are in there, take this tip from my friend Regena:

> "When doing a good toilet cleaning, don't forget the bolt covers on your seat. Pop those open, pour in a little peroxide, and poof, no more, *Where is that urinal smell coming from?*"

While we're on the fascinating topic of toilets…one day, early in our marriage, I was complaining about how hard it was to get our toilet seat clean. My sexy husband came home with three brand-new toilet seats—one for each throne in our house. When I protested (we were broke and I didn't want to spend all that money on new fixtures), he showed me the price tags; each seat was under ten dollars. We kept the toilet seats. Every couple of years we replace all the seats in the house. It's a great way to keep your bathroom fresh for not a lot of money.

In bathrooms it's important to work from the top down. And then wipe your way out of the room. It will look great and you'll have the satisfaction of knowing that you've given your housemates and yourself the gift of a clean bathroom.

Step 4: Label It and Put It Away

In my tiny under-the-sink area, I have two pullout drawers on the bottom and two open plastic containers on top. One drawer is labeled "Travel Stuff"; the other drawer is labeled "Supplies," for all those things I don't want to run out of in the middle of my bathroom time (extra razors, one extra bath gel, shampoo, conditioner, deodorant).

One plastic container is labeled "Hair" for my hair dryer, brushes, and favorite curling iron—only those hair products that I use when I'm blow-drying or curling my hair. The other container is "Girl Stuff," an important bin to keep filled with a teenage girl in the house.

I store my now totally fresh makeup in a clear acrylic countertop beauty organizer. It's easy to see what's there and what isn't, and it makes getting made-up less of a hide-and-seek mission in the morning.

Obviously, your bins and drawers or shelves are going to be different from mine. My goal is that when my kid calls from another room, "Mom, where is the…" I can actually tell them where it is.

Step 5: Keep It Up

I don't care if you have six bathrooms and are on one of those reality shows where you have two dozen kids who do all the cleaning. Every bathroom should be stocked with its own toilet-bowl scrub brush, its own container of wipes for quick cleans (or a bottle of cleanser and a roll of paper towels), and its own glass cleaner. Period.

That way, in less than five minutes you can have the bathroom "family clean." Family clean is the level of cleaning needed when my family members, my best friends, or the kids' friends are over. Sadly, a different level of cleaning is still required for "proper company" and mothers-in-law.

> "I always used the kids' bath time to clean the bathroom—
> since I had to be in there anyway. I also do a quick swipe of
> the bathroom sink and counter while waiting for the shower
> to warm up, and while I have conditioner on my hair, I wipe
> down the shower walls with a washcloth (or shave my legs,
> whichever area looks more desperate)."—Susan

Keeping the STEM Strong

Space

This is the area where I feel most challenged in my bathroom, so I've had to find some space-saving solutions to make every square inch work for me.

Storage hooks. I'm a big believer in hooks all over the house. The hooks in my bathroom get a lot of use with all my necklaces. I keep them in my bathroom because that's the last thing I put on as I'm walking out the bathroom door.

In a kids' bathroom, towel hooks instead of racks make a lot of sense. Anything that causes a kid to have to take more than two seconds to accomplish will probably be ignored. If they can just put their towel on a hook instead of having to fumble with a rack, the percentage of hang-ups will go way up.

Remember the walls. If counter space is at a premium, think about your wall space. Roger mounted a magnifying mirror on our bathroom wall so it wouldn't take up the kind of counter space we don't have. Plus it's mounted at a level that actually has good light, and I don't have to squat when plucking that stray eyebrow hair.

Temporary holders.

> "I need somewhere to stash my jewelry when I take it off. I do
> have a permanent place for it, but I usually take it off when I

get in the shower and think I'm going to put it right back on, so I leave it out. A little cup or finger bowl is just right to prevent it from getting wet or knocked into the toilet. Then I can put it back on after my shower or back into the jewelry box. We also have an over the door row of hooks on which we hang robes or lightly used gym clothes that will be used again."—Rita

Time

Color by kids. When we had three kids living at home at the same time (and all sharing one bathroom), it was important to be able to keep each of their things straight. We let each kid pick a color (Justen was green, Jeremy was red, and Kimberly was blue), and then gave them towels, washcloths, and toothbrushes in those colors. That way, no one could steal the other person's towel, and when we saw a green towel on the bathroom floor, we knew which kid was responsible. When we switched to an electric toothbrush, we made sure to get the brush heads in the kids' assigned colors.

As for things like hairbrushes and styling products, you can use hair rubber bands in the appropriate colors to distinguish one black brush from another. Besides staying organized, it can cut down on family feuds as well.

> "With five kids, I dealt with endless complaints about stolen towels and never having clean, dry towels when they got out of the shower. Until I bought five different colored towels. Now I know right away who didn't hang their towel to dry or left it crumpled on the floor. And their bathroom looks bright and cheery all decked out in rainbow colors."—Renee

Laundry hampers. Everyone should have a laundry hamper in the room they get undressed in (or close by in the hall.) If you have room in your bathroom, that's a great place for a hamper. Kids (and adults) are much more likely to use the hamper if it's right there.

Energy

Washcloths. Ever since I had my own tiny apartment, I've had bath towels with matching hand towels and washcloths. But the washcloths kept getting stained with makeup when I washed my face at night. Finally, I bought twenty white washcloths at Target. I can bleach them until they are white again, and they get the job done.

Toilet paper. Every bathroom should have an ample supply of TP within easy reach (but not on the floor right beside the toilet, as I soon learned after having a little boy). Depending on the layout of your bathroom, store extra toilet paper:

- On the back of the toilet tank
- In a pretty basket next to the sink
- Under the sink
- On a shelf in the bathroom

Correct aim.

> "I had a vinyl expression (sticker) placed on the inner lid of my son's toilet that said, 'Please AIM here.' It had an arrow pointing down. A nice reminder that I didn't have to verbalize."—Jenny

Money

Product junkie. Earlier this year I challenged myself not to buy any beauty products for six months. Instead of hitting Bath and Body when I was out of my favorite shower gel, I forced myself to look through all my cupboards and use the stuff I received for Christmas and birthdays. Not my favorite scents, but perfectly acceptable and free.

One of your biggest money savers is to use what you already have.

Bonus Projects

TOWELS

- I once stayed in a hotel where the bathroom had a small basket with rolled-up washcloths tucked inside. It looked so clean and pretty and gave me a lot of joy to look at. It didn't occur to me for weeks afterward that it would take nothing but a basket to do the same thing in my own bathroom.

- Oh bath sheets, where have you been all my life? If you like to be wrapped up in a towel and have some room to spare, get yourself a bath sheet. You will definitely want a hook to hang it on, but it is so worth it!

THINK OUTSIDE THE BOWL

I was given a pretty black-and-cream bowl with different translations of the word *live* on the inside. I adore the bowl, but it just didn't look right in my red, green, and gold kitchen. Finally, I realized that just because it's a bowl doesn't mean it needs to be in the kitchen. It looks great in our upstairs bathroom and is the perfect container for holding all my pairs of glasses.

I've done similar things in other bathrooms. I have some depression glass that looks great in our girly downstairs bath, some picture frames on the walls of our master bath, and other fun stuff tucked into corners.

Project Reports

"I *loved* the tips regarding kids. I will be installing hooks in the other bathrooms in my house because they *always* drop towels on the floor, as they are too young and short to reach the towel bars easily. I also plan to color code each kid's towels and put all the girls' hair accessories in those shoe holders organized by color. *Genius.*"—Wendy

Project 4

Kids' Rooms

The goal of organizing a kid's room is not to have a clean room.

Let that sink in for a minute.

I know that you would trade any amount of money to not cringe when you walked by your daughter's room. I would have as well. It took me years and tears to realize that the goal was not to have a clean room. The goal was to raise a self-reliant kid in that room.

That meant finding a system that worked for my daughter, not for me. None of my kids, while under voting age, would ever receive the Clean Room Award. Even now, with only one child living at home, I still close the door as I walk by his room.

However, when Justen needs to find a pot of paint, a book, or Super Glue in his room, he doesn't have to tear the room apart. He knows where everything is. It may look like chaos, but it's orderly chaos in Justen's world.

Justen goes to school full-time as well as working three full days a week. He hosts a game day at our house every Sunday afternoon for a bunch of his friends, and he does chores without grumbling (mostly). So who am I to say that his room isn't working for him?

However, if my goal were just to make sure that Justen had a clean room, I could have easily gone in and cleaned it to my standards. However, a clean room is not my goal. My goal is to have my future daughter-in-law rise up and call me blessed.

So going into this chapter knowing that our goal is to have self-reliant kids, here are some suggestions from me and from some of the best train-up-a-child moms I know. In this area, it's important to try some different systems. If they fail, that's fine. Not every suggestion is going to work for every family (or even every kid in every family). Find something that fits you and make adjustments from there.

Step 1: Your Plan of Attack

The very first thing you have to do when considering a plan for organizing and maintaining your kids' quarters is to get the model-home-kids'-bedroom picture out of your head. If you want your kids' rooms to be the first stop on your Cosmopolitan Living Home Tour, please skip this chapter.

However, if you want a room where your kids

- can sleep peacefully at night
- will want to curl up with a good book
- can express who they are with their rooms
- can easily get dressed in the morning
- will learn the basics of maintaining an organized space of their own

then this chapter is for you.

Remember Rule 5: "Treat Your Home like a Grown-Up Kindergarten Room." Nowhere does that apply more than in your child's space. Anything you want your child to be responsible to maintain (or even help be responsible to maintain) needs to be in plain sight, clearly marked, and at a kid level.

Yes, you can store things under your kid's bed, but just realize that no kid is going to pull out under-bed storage tubs and put things away. (The only exception might be if your daughter is hiding a diary down there.) Storage in out-of-the-way places has to be for things that Mom is going to need to access: out-of-season clothes, extra bedding, and so on.

The next step in your plan of attack is figuring out what the issues in this room are. In this case, you need an expert's opinion, so ask your child. Some of their frustrations you already know: a meltdown occurs every morning about what to wear to school; he's constantly losing bits and pieces of his favorite toys; her room has a way of eating library books.

Maybe your son really does want to have a clear space, but doesn't know how. Maybe your daughter's one real hope is to have a reading nook in the corner of her room, but there isn't space.

Find out what your kid's hopes are for the room. If he knows that you're working hard with him to create a space to keep his comic book collection out of the destructive hands of his four-year-old brother, you're going to have a much more willing partner in getting the room in order.

Step 2: Sort It Out

> "My daughters share a room, and it was a disaster. In the end, I realized that we allowed them to have too much stuff. Purging was the only thing that helped."—Becky

When it comes to actually picking up the room, introduce your kids to the three-box, two-bag system, with some modification so they don't get overwhelmed. While cleaning with your kids, set a timer for five minutes, and then see how much you can both do as a team in that time. I love Adelle's approach to making the mess manageable:

> "When my eight-year-old cleans his room, I tell him to start with one item at a time. For example, I'll say, 'Pick up and put away all the books you can find. Now, pick up all the loose papers and decide what to keep and what to throw away. Next, find all the stuffed animals and put them in their basket.' It's less overwhelming when he's faced with a really chaotic room to clean."

OTHER ROOMS

For kids, I encourage you to put away the things in the "Other

Rooms" box as soon as you get to a certain number of items. You could use the child's age as the magic number, so when the six-year-old has six items or the ten-year-old ten, he can put stuff away around the house. That way, it gives you a natural break in the activity of cleaning the room.

PUT BACK

Hold on to this box until you've made some organizing decisions in the "Label It and Put It Away" step.

GIVE AWAY

Often it's not the kids who have a hard time getting rid of stuff, it's the parents:

- "I paid a lot for that toy."
- "Her aunt Lucy gave that to her."
- "She may want to use it someday."
- "He'll want to keep it to remember preschool."

We weigh our kids down with our own emotional baggage.

My daughter, Kimber, was great at getting rid of stuff—books she was no longer reading, clothes she was no longer wearing, stuffed animals she no longer cared about. Every time I saw one of her childhood stuffed friends or the unworn shirt her grandma gave her for Christmas end up in the Goodwill bag, I hesitated. It just didn't feel right to get rid of it.

I had to realize that she was getting rid of things to make room for the life she currently had. She saved in the attic a few of her favorite stuffed animals, and she still wore a lot of the other clothes Grandma had given her, but she wanted to get rid of the things that were no longer serving her.

Remember our criteria for keeping and giving away an item? Teach your kids to think through these things:

- Is it something they currently use or wear?
- Is it something that makes them happy when they see it?
- Is it something they will definitely use in the next six months?

If they can't answer yes to at least one of these questions, it either needs to be given away or put away in another room or, in a few rare situations, stored away.

I've made an index card with this list for when I'm cleaning out a space. Perhaps your child's own index card would be a great help in letting go of some treasures.

GARBAGE AND RECYCLING

Kids are learning about the environment every day at school. This is an excellent time to talk about what they can do to recycle.

Step 3: Clean It Up

Now that you have some cleared-off surfaces, it's time for your team to do some cleaning. This is where some "fun" cleaning supplies can come in handy with younger kids.

Make sure everyone has an apron. Younger kids can have a cowboy apron with holsters for the cleaning supplies or fairy princess tutus with a magic wand feather duster. Allow them to wear them only while cleaning. Some other fun cleaning accessories could include:

- A feather duster
- Cleaning rags in festive colors
- A squirt bottle filled with organic general household cleaner
- A bucket with your child's name painted on it to hold all the supplies

Give kids cleaning tasks that are appropriate for their ages. I especially like the idea of sending smaller kids under beds and into corners of closets to get things cleaned out. God made 'em small for a reason.

Step 4: Label It and Put It Away

Here are some of the best (and most effective) storage ideas from some professional moms (and a dad!):

Clothes. Organize your kids' clothing on a separate day from your organization of the rest of their room. Younger kids are going to need you to make most of the decisions for them, and older kids are going to make their input known. When you do get to organizing all the clothes, pull out those three boxes and two bags, but add in one more box: "hand-me-downs."

Now go through the system with your kids' clothes:

HAND-ME-DOWNS

If you have younger kids that will be wearing big brother's too-small jammies, this is the box that they go into. (You can decide later if they go straight into another child's drawers, or in the basement to be stored for another birthday or two.)

OTHER ROOMS

This box is for out-of-season clothes that will still fit next season, and anything that doesn't belong in your child's clothes drawers. You will transfer all out-of-season clothes into a box for storage (high up on a closet shelf or under their bed).

PUT BACK

Place in this box any clothes you still want to have available, but they're just in the wrong spot.

GIVE AWAY

Your last child has grown out of size twos. Put any clothes of that size in this box and offer it to the mom at church, the crisis pregnancy center in your town, or the charity of your choice.

GARBAGE AND RECYCLING

You won't let your kids wear their Veggie Tales shirt because of a stubborn ketchup stain that never came out. Well, no other mom wants her kids to wear it either. In most communities, you can recycle old, clean clothes that are no longer wearable.

Closets. Keep that garbage bag close for any trash you find in the closet. I've been shocked at the things I've found, especially in boys' closets.

> "I keep labeled tubs in my kids closets, so when they outgrow clothes, I can move them into the tubs easily and keep their drawers and closets from getting too full and keep my kids from trying to wear something that's too small for them. I keep my kids' off-season clothes on a shelf in their closet in case we get unseasonable weather (out of the way, but still accessible). This came in really handy last week when we had rain and hail (even a tornado warning) in sunny California in June!"—Janell

Or, if you have enough hanging space in your closets:

> "I have started hanging my boys' clothes in outfits (shirts and bottoms) so it is easier to choose an outfit that matches. I also hang the season we are in on the lower bar, with the off-season on the higher bar. That way, if we need an outfit for an unseasonable day, they are there, but the ones in arm's reach are the correct season. This also helps minimize arguments about what to wear."—Dawn

TOY MANAGEMENT

A Toy Library

> "Turn a closet into a toy closet. All toys are stored in organized, labeled containers, and kids can play with only one bin of toys at a time. They have to turn in one bin before they can play with another."—Alexia

Stuffed Animals

"A toy hammock is a great idea. The kids can just toss stuffed animals up there and off the floor."—Robin

A Million Little Pieces

"I think I should write a book called *101 Uses for an Over-the-Door Shoe Organizer.* They work for toys too, especially for a girl's room. Think Barbies, Barbie clothes, Polly Pockets, and so on. Avoid toy boxes or anything deep that can become the chasm of hopelessness. Toys go in, but they don't come out (well, not until you've thrown away every other part to the toy, *then* it shows up!)."—Robin

"I'm a Lego organizer freak these days—directions and pieces all in a see-through container with a label on the box. I keep them on a high shelf so I control access to them, and the bins make for an easy cleanup. I have let go of perfect separation of toys. As long as the boys are happy and can find their stuff, I'm happy."—Stephanie

Less Is More

"Fewer toys equals more attention focused on what my kids do have. Have your children pick three or four favorites at a birthday or Christmas and put the rest out of sight. When their interest starts to fade with, say, the tea set Aunt June got them, put it in the closet and pull out the box of dress-up that Grandma sent. Every three months or so we switch out toys. Right now it's dress-up, art tower, four board games, and Legos."—Christy

"Spring cleaning happens every season at our house. After birthdays and Christmas, we also have a Donation Station where my kids can search through their piles of toys and other things that have accumulated and give them to the Salvation Army or other charity. We throw them in a huge bag and donate away."—Jenny

"Each birthday and Christmas the boys have to 'give to others who have less than they do.' For every new toy that comes in, one goes out. It's a lesson on giving, and it curbs the overabundance of stuff."—Stephanie

Step 5: Keep It Up

ALL THAT ARTWORK

"I would love to know what to do with all of my kids' artwork," Jenny said. "They have tons of artwork and projects that come home with them, but I can't keep everything—I have three kids! I read of someone who took pictures of their kids' school projects and then put them in books, but I hardly have time to go to the bathroom, let alone take pictures of artwork."

If you don't want to go the picture route, here's my simple solution for kids' art:

1. Get a clear tub to put under their bed.

2. Write the school year on the back of any artwork you want to keep.

3. Start putting those precious pictures in the box (you'll probably fill it up in the kindergarten year alone).

4. Over the coming years, you'll get better at weeding out the artwork that's "expendable." Force yourself to go through it regularly and get rid of the pieces you don't want to hang on to for a lifetime.

5. As the years progress, you'll have less and less stuff that makes it into the box, unless your child is planning to major in art in college. Then you're on your own.

And what to do with all those precious pieces that haven't earned a right in the box? Here are some suggestions:

• Turn it into a card and send it to Grandma.

- Create a laundry-room art gallery or homework spotlight by putting up a clothesline and rotating the art you display on it.

- My friend Melissa had a frame in her kitchen that featured sticky paper instead of a picture so she could easily attach or remove her kids' art on it.

- Use a different child's artwork each night as a centerpiece on the table.

Keeping the STEM Strong

Space

"If kids are old enough, often a loft bed is a great choice. You can get one with a desk underneath as well, to save lots of space."—Robin

Time

MORNING MADNESS

"I would have the kids' clothes picked out and put in bins labeled 'Monday,' 'Tuesday,' etc. It was easy getting ready for school—no hassle trying to find socks or a matching T-shirt. Each kid had their own set of weekly bins. I also had a hook-and-bin area for backpacks and homework. Before bed, everything had to be found and put in the right spot so that mornings went smoothly. With five little ones, you *have* to be organized."—Carrie

I love the bin idea because it's out in the open and easy for kids to access. I also love Peta's idea below. Yes, it's hidden in a closet, but what a great way to simplify your child's morning routine (and yours).

"Organization is a special need for my son. I use a hanging wardrobe organizer with several compartments and label each compartment with the days of the week. I put his clothes into the organizer straight from the laundry, a full set including undies for each day. I clip a peg onto the compartment for 'today' because that's another challenge for him (and also for me some days). He grabs today's set, moves the peg to the next day (sometimes), and voilà, an end to the clothes-all-over-the-floor, search-for-a-sock drama. Pj's go in the side pocket of this container. I place his other clothes into his drawers to cycle in another week. This system works for our daughter too."—Peta

Energy

"Put a basketball hoop above the clothes hamper. Make it a game."—Brian

"Each of my kids is color coded. They each have their own laundry basket and hangers in their own color. They know which basket is theirs to take from or put away, and since they share closets, they know which clothes are theirs by the color of their hangers. I love the color system. Even little kids can figure it out."—Stephanie

Money

Hand-Me-Downs

"With three boys, we use the dot system. Our oldest gets one permanent-marker dot on the tag of each of his clothes, middle son gets two dots, and third gets three dots. When something is passed down, it's so easy just to add a little dot, and I don't have to try to remember what belongs to whom."—Jessica

Bonus Projects

Kids, even if they share a room, need a space all their own, even if it's just a bed chair that no one else is allowed to touch. After cleaning up, find something special for your child that says, "This is all yours."

Project Reports

"I love the three-box, two-bag idea. It puts words and defini-tions on how to help our kids move through their rooms to clean them. It cuts down on that overwhelmed feeling that our kids get when faced with their rooms. I think that our children (middle-school ages) will be able to carry this system forward as a habit in their own homes. We're good housekeepers in general, especially given that we have three kids and two dogs! But we do get a little bogged down in stuff that isn't where it should be, so this will help us all."—Sharon

Project 5

Your Kitchen

I love my kitchen. It's warm and cozy and decorated in rich Tuscan colors. I love it so much that I don't often think about it. Recently, I was looking at the red hutch in the eating area (which looks so cool in my golden-yellow kitchen) and realized it has become a junk collection site.

I love some things on it. My mom's old coffee grinder (that my brother and I used to grind dog food in, and my mom promptly retired from the coffee-grinding business), the three fat chickens Roger and I bought on a bed-and-breakfast tour of Northern California, and some cute Disney coffee canisters (yes, some people in this house are Disney freaks). I love all of those things. But I totally forgot they were there because there was so much other stuff to contend with—little trinkets that had accumulated and that I didn't love, but didn't do a darn thing about.

For your project today, I want you to keep all those things you love and use in your kitchen, and ditch the rest.

Step 1: Your Plan of Attack

Unless your kitchen is the size of a sailboat galley, you're probably going to want to divide this project into different areas. Don't worry about food right now; let's just get the rest of the kitchen into shape, and we can deal with the food when we talk about shopping. So leave your fridge, food cabinets, and pantry for another day.

Take the kitchen one cabinet at a time. Grab your timer, put some great, upbeat music on your iPod, get some rags and surface cleaner, and let's go to town.

The most important part of organizing your kitchen is to not get sidetracked. Even if you come across your grandma's recipe for apple bread and see a bunch of apples sitting right there, resist the temptation! Keep going.

Oh, and don't try to bake four dozen cookies for the bake sale while you're cleaning out your cabinets. Cooking a pot roast? Fine, but if you have two timers going off every twelve and fifteen minutes, my guess is you're going to have a chaotic kitchen and some charcoal-like chocolate-chip cookies.

Reclaim Some Counter Space

I'm passionate about the need for clear counter space in a kitchen. Nothing should be on the counter that doesn't either: (1) work regularly for you, or (2) make you happy when you look at it. My coffee-maker sees more action than the funnel-cake stand at a county fair, so it deserves a place on the counter. My food processor I use only once a week or so. It has not earned the right to be on the counter.

I have to fight regularly with my stuff to keep it off the counter. I promise you, clutter and appliances migrate there in the middle of the night. I am constantly waging a battle to keep my counters cleared.

Here's a list of things that have not earned the right to be there (but keep trying to sneak their way on):

- Slow cooker
- Can opener
- Kids' school projects
- Dishes that just don't want to get put away
- Mail

Things that have earned the right to be on my counter:

- Coffeemaker

- Canisters (they're not just decorative, they hold everyday essentials like coffee filters, packets of sweetener, and dog treats)

- Toaster oven (so we don't need to fire up the big oven very often)

- Spices

- Container of frequently used utensils

- Butcher block of knives

- Toaster

Your use of counter space is going to be different from mine, but you get the idea—be thoughtful about what you allow to live on your counter.

Another great counter space saver is to see what you can mount under your cabinets or on your walls. For the longest time, I had a vertical paper-towel rack that sat on the counter. I was constantly frustrated since it took up so much space. Then one day, it occurred to me that just because our house wasn't built with an under-counter towel rack didn't mean I couldn't do the job myself (or bribe my cute husband to do it with a plateful of chocolate-chip cookies). I also have a microwave and CD player/radio mounted under my cabinets to save space.

On my walls, I have a cute set of stainless-steel measuring spoons and a coffee scoop. I use them every day, they look great on the walls, and everyone in my house knows where to put them away. Another space-saving idea is a magnetic knife holder mounted on the wall.

I'm sure as you look around your kitchen or browse in a kitchen-gadgets store, you'll think of other creative ways to clear your counters.

Step 2: Sort It Out

You got it—three boxes and two bags. But this time with a twist! If your kitchen is tiny and you're clamoring for cupboard space, I want you to grab an extra storage box for all those dishes, plates, and roasting pans you use only on special occasions. Some items might include:

- Giant platters (especially if they have a turkey motif)

- Extra casserole dishes (Do you really need more than three in your cupboards?)

- Cake stands

- Extra dishes

Anything you don't use weekly but do use for bigger occasions (Christmas, Easter, Thanksgiving, Passover, birthdays) goes into this tub.

OTHER ROOMS

Our kitchen is a multipurpose room, so anything that has wandered from its correct home—papers, game pieces, books—goes in this box. Then I redistribute them around the house (or assign some child to do it). When I remind our kids to clean up, I would say only 85 percent of the cleaning job usually happens. Yes, in a perfect world, kids would clean everything up all the time. In a perfect world, so would I. I'm still waiting.

Mail tends to migrate into our kitchen (it's the first room you hit on the way back from our mailbox). Make sure your mail has a designated place in the kitchen or that it quickly goes into the room it's supposed to be in.

PUT BACK

Save these for after you Clean It Up.

GIVE AWAY

If you have a child who's setting up a house in the next year, you have my permission to put aside extra pans, pots, utensils, and dishes you're no longer using. If your child is in junior high, you do not have my permission and must donate all those items. Other excuses that are not valid for keeping those pots and pans you hate:

- "We may get a camper someday." But why would you want to make cooking harder when you're camping? We have one decent pot, one decent fry pan, a campfire coffee-maker, and some utensils that we all like to use and are easy to clean up.

- "My baby's going off to college." Again, congrats. But they aren't allowed to cook in their dorms.

- "Somebody might need them someday." You're cor-rect. Many people need them, and that's why you should donate your extras.

GARBAGE AND RECYCLING

This is obvious. Get rid of anything that someone else would not be blessed with.

Step 3: Clean It Up

Take a multipurpose cleaner and wipe down shelves, doors, pull-outs, and so on.

Step 4: Label It and Put It Away

Each of your cabinets should have a purpose and a label, even if the label is just in your head. Each drawer should store a certain type of item.

Yes, we have cabinets for drinkware. The mugs go on one shelf, the drinking glasses on another. That way, whoever is putting away dishes (usually a kid) knows exactly where things go.

If you have younger kids, you may want to actually label the shelves so kids can help put things away. You'll most likely want to place the labels on the inside of the cabinet, but every time your child gets their own cup, plate, or napkin, those labels will help reinforce where things go. The goal is to be able to tell a stranger, from another room, where something is in your kitchen.

This is the time to create a space for your tub of special occasion platters, roasting pans, etc. We have a shelf in our garage near the Christmas items where ours is stored 355 days a year. Think about a spot in your basement, a high shelf in your pantry, or another out-of-the-way storage spot.

Step 5: Keep It Up

Be vigilant about keeping things off your counters. You are allowed one junk drawer, but as soon as it: (1) is impossible to find things in there, or (2) won't shut properly, it's time to clean it out. Use the three-box, two-bag system for cleaning out your junk drawer while you watch TV.

Keeping the STEM Strong

Space

My friend Shannon was tired of her husband's stuff always being all over the kitchen (mail he needed to look at, his phone charger, and so on). Finally, Shannon got a little basket and labeled it "Steve's Stuff." When Steve knows it's for him, he actually deals with it or puts it back into the basket. Win!

Time

Even if you just have a few minutes, you can use that time to organize a cabinet:

> "I just did my plastic-container cabinet. It's been an open-the-door-and-chuck-it kind of area, so it was lovely to take it all apart and find the three things that have both container and lid. I filled a grocery bag with mismatched lids that will never find their mate and put those in the recycling bin. It took maybe three minutes, and I'm already inspired!

I think I'll tackle one cabinet a day and get them done right away."—Shannon

Energy

When Roger and I first got married, we bought one of those plate stands (like you would serve English tea on) plus twenty-four clear glass plates at IKEA for two dollars each so that when we have a gang of people over, we never have to worry about having enough plates that are appropriate. We may buy some festive napkins for a birthday celebration, but by not using disposable plates, we're creating less trash, saving money, and the plates look great. (It's funny to see our puggle, Jake, lose his mind when we have the glass plates on our glass patio table. He can't understand why he keeps bonking his nose when he tries to snatch the steak that's *right there*.)

Money

It makes sense to spend a little money making your kitchen a place you want to be. It's an investment worth making. If your kitchen is cluttered, you're going to be less inclined to want to spend time in there cooking, and takeout and drive-thrus start to add up. Here are a couple of low-cost ways to brighten up your space:

- Frame a couple pictures of you and your husband, your kids, or your dog and hang them on the walls.

- Buy a lemony hand soap to keep at your sink.

- Keep a pair of iPod speakers in the kitchen.

- Buy an herb-scented candle to burn while you're cleaning.

Bonus Projects

"Because we have such a small kitchen and not much counter space, I had very little room whenever I used a cookbook, and it would constantly get splattered with whatever I was making. So finally my husband got me a cookbook holder that attaches underneath the kitchen cabinets. I just pull it down, place my cookbook on it, and voilà, the cookbook's off the counter. And the holder folds out of the way nicely. It's the best present my husband ever got me!"—Kristina

Project Reports

"The extra box is a really good idea. I think I need a box for items I use just for entertaining—platters, drink dispenser, cupcake stand, etc. I also need an extra box for paperware/plasticware. We keep these on hand for when we have people over or for birthday parties and special events, and they tend to migrate into the kitchen drawers and cabinets."—Jennifer

Project 6

Your Office/Hobby Area

At first, I was going to write two separate chapters—one for your office and the other for your hobby area. However, if you're like me and many of my friends, it can sometimes be hard to figure out where your hobby leaves off and where your business begins.

For a dozen years, I (and the IRS) called my writing a hobby. Now it has become a business. But at first, the needs were the same: a desk to write at (or a clean dinner table, coffee table, or back patio), a file box, and a few supplies.

Maybe you started your eBay business as a hobby to sell off your collection of porcelain frogs that, weirdly, people kept giving you even though you don't like frogs or porcelain. Now you're the Frog Queen of eBay.

I know that home businesses grow out of wanting a paycheck from doing what we love. That's why a home office and hobby area often can't be separated. But even if you don't work from home or have a hobby that requires stuff, you probably still need a scaled-down office to keep on top of life.

It's great if you can have a whole room dedicated as your office/ grown-up playroom/craft room/sewing room/studio/workroom. However, as I write this, my sixth book, I have five employees and still don't have an office. A girl, sometimes, has to make do.

Our bedroom makes sense for my office. It has more space than we need and stays cooler than the other rooms in the house in the summer.

We do have another office in the house, but Roger has that. (Yes, we both work from home. All prayers are accepted.) Sometimes, when my team of employees is over, I move my laptop to the kitchen table, and we work from there.

Figure out where your space makes sense.

Step 1: Your Plan of Attack

Wherever your office or workspace is, make sure it's functional and attractive.

When you look through organizing magazines, those photographers are trying to trick you by saying, "Of course you can run your entire business from an antique hutch in your kitchen. So what if it doesn't have any drawer space and half of your laptop will hang over the opening of the hutch so you have to balance it on your knees. Look how fun and funky it looks!"

Step away from the magazine.

Your space has to be functional first. If it's inconvenient, you're going to leave your stuff all over the place, and you'll be in more of a mess than if you didn't have any space at all.

Each person's need for functionality is going to be different. If you're a quilter (like my mom), apparently you'll need giant tables and enough closet space to house the contents of a Jo-Ann Fabric and Craft store.

Here are the basics of what most workspaces need:

- A good chair (probably on rollers)
- A worktable
- A basket to dump papers that need to be dealt with
- A cup with plenty of pens, pencils, and scissors that work
- Space for your laptop
- File drawers
- Plenty of file folders for all those papers

- Garbage and recycling baskets (because most of those papers can probably be recycled)

Step 2: Sort It Out

It's important to keep this area clear. If you have to wade through a wad of papers, move stacks of folded clothes, or clean up before you work, you're going to have plenty of excuses to not work or to do that hobby you love instead.

OTHER ROOMS

Clear out anything that doesn't belong in your workspace. This especially includes other people's stuff.

PUT BACK

Put anything in this box that needs a place in your workspace but has wandered from its intended spot.

GIVE AWAY

If you're trying to support too many hobbies at once, this is an excellent box to focus on.

For years I worked (and played) with rubber stamps. But when I lost interest, I lost interest fast. I had hundreds of (if not a couple thousand) dollars' worth of stamps and supplies. Because I wasn't using them, however, they were worthless.

Finally, after a year of not touching any of my supplies, I had a choice: sell them or give them away. I do not have a good track record for selling things. You have to be all in to make any money on those ventures. I've had some wildly successful garage sales in the past, but I knew that people were going to be looking to buy those stamps for pennies on the dollar.

In the end, I gave all the stamps except for a couple (a bookplate stamp and a "thank you" stamp) to a woman at church who made cards for church members and friends. Yes, I missed a few bucks, but it was so much cooler to be able to see all those materials put to good use.

GARBAGE AND RECYCLING

Things in business and crafts change quickly. The magazines that were inspiring five years ago are out-of-date now. Get rid of or shred any papers that no longer serve you.

Step 3: Clean It Up

Give the area a good cleaning. Dust out drawers, clean off shelves, and make it shine. The goal is to make the area so inviting, you want to sit down there and work.

Step 4: Label It and Put It Away

If you are using files, cubbies, or lidless boxes, remember Rule 5: "Treat Your Home like a Grown-Up Kindergarten Room."

> "Like most scrapbookers, I'm a little behind in my scrapbooking. Therefore, after any event that needs to go in the book, any photos and paraphernalia (tickets, postcards, brochures) go into a file folder at the back of a plastic box. When I have time to scrapbook, I grab the folder in the front, and I'm ready to add a page. Someday I'll scrapbook faster than I add files and get caught up!"—Renee

> "I have bins for my scrapbooking, sewing, and knitting. When I have a project, I put everything I'm going to use in a basket. That way I can grab the basket and work on it."—Jamie

Step 5: Keep It Up

The best way to keep this space clear is to regularly invite people over for a work or hobby night. Don't underestimate the power of public humiliation when it comes to an area that it would be just as easy to shut the door on.

Also, keep the area pretty. Put in your personal touches so that it's a place you want to keep organized and easy to use.

Keeping the STEM Strong

Space

If you have overindulged in office supplies, keep a bucket in your garage or basement of extras that you're currently not using. That way, your office stays clutter free, and you can go shopping in your basement the next time you need tape.

Time

Have a list of commonly used supplies taped up in your room so the next time you go to the office supply store, you won't forget anything you may need and have to make another trip. Here's a list of items my friend Linda keeps in her office drawers:

Envelopes (standard size)	Sharpies
Business envelopes	Markers
5 x 7 envelopes	Crayons
8.5 x 11 envelopes	Pencils
Paper clips	Batteries
Clamps	Tape
Rubber bands	Glue
Stamps	Computer CDs (blank)
Wite-Out	Address book
Scissors	Extension cords
Sticky notes	Flashlights
Index cards	

Energy

When you have a home office, it's easy to be distracted by little chores, Facebook, the dog, the fridge, everything around you.

One thing that has helped me as I sit down to write or work is to light a candle next to me. The candle signifies to my family that I am on the clock, and unless there's a fire or blood, think twice about interrupting me.

However, the biggest advantage the candle provides is in focusing me. I never want to leave a burning candle unattended, so I think twice about getting up from the desk and blowing it out, knowing I'll have to relight it when I get back. Every time I light the candle, I pray for the work I need to do, and that God would grant me the creativity to communicate what he has put on my heart in a way that is winsome to women.

Money

I have an addiction to office supplies—pens and pencils and Post-its, oh my!

Every couple of months I challenge myself to stay out of the office supply store for thirty days. This forces me to find all those supplies that have wandered throughout the house and now need to come home.

Project 7

Garages and Basements

"Schadenfreude" is pleasure derived from the misfortunes of others. I had heard the term before, but had never experienced it until Carol told me about her messy garage.

You see, Carol, a friend and fellow writer, is one of those people who just naturally organizes anything she lays her hands on. (I really don't understand her kind of people.) However, when I discovered not everything was perfect in Carol's world, I got the tiniest sense of pleasure. Here's Carol's story in her own words:

> "I knew it was time to get serious with garage organization the day my husband came home from work and announced, 'We have twenty thousand dollars' worth of cars sitting in the driveway and two hundred dollars' worth of junk filling up the garage. What's wrong with this picture?' We always entered and left the house through the garage, and seeing all that junk at least twice a day was more than a little depressing."

See! Organized people can be a mess just like the rest of us! And yes, I know God still has a lot of work to do with me. Therefore, as part of my healing process, I've asked Carol to help me offer some tips and ideas from her now-tidy garage. These ideas apply to any large space you will be sorting and organizing: garage, basement, storage units, and in one of my friend's cases, a barn.

Step 1: Your Plan of Attack

What you will need:

- Your three boxes and two bags
- Blue painter's tape
- Permanent markers
- A legal pad
- Sheet protectors

But first, a caution. The following words should never come out of your mouth: "I need to organize the garage." Utter those words and *boom*, you are already defeated. You should never try to organize that space all at once. It is vital that you divide the area up and work on only one section at a time. Here are some areas you may want to consider:

- Sports equipment
- Camping equipment
- Storage
- Christmas storage
- Tools
- Gardening
- Hobby
- Out-of-season clothes

You probably have other areas in your garage as well. List them all on your legal pad and organize them one section at a time.

Step 2: Sort It Out

After you've picked the section you'll be working on, set up your three boxes and two bags. If you're sorting through a lot of boxes and storage containers, here's one trick that has helped me keep track of what's been gone through and what hasn't: Once I go through a box, I label it with blue tape and the permanent marker. Any boxes that don't have blue tape on them still need to be gone through.

OTHER ROOMS

"Group like kinds of supplies—painting tools, yard tools, sporting equipment, auto supplies—and store them where you can easily see them," Carol advises. "Clear plastic containers work well for this. Keep the ones you use most often up front and easily accessible."

So if your sporting equipment is taking up residence with your gardening tools, put it in the "Other Rooms" box; don't leave it where it doesn't belong.

PUT BACK

"If your garage lacks storage," Carol says, "invest in some shelving for the side walls. Be sure to measure so you still have room for those cars to fit!"

In our garage, we have library-style shelving, and now any storage boxes that we purchase are the clear kind so it's easy to see the contents. And the boxes and shelving make it easier to put things back.

GIVE AWAY

Our garage is the place where hopes and dreams go to die. The golf clubs you had to have but used only once, your husband's someday project of restoring an engine, your kid's Beanie Baby collection—give that stuff away. It's a crime when things that others could be using and loving become a tripping hazard in your home.

GARBAGE AND RECYCLING

Once a year, we schedule a trip to the dump for all those things we can't donate, recycle, or store in our garage. (Conveniently, our dump now takes dead computers and other electronics to recycle them.) That dump trip always comes the day after cleaning out the garage.

Step 3: Clean It Up

If your stuff is important enough for you to keep, it's important enough for you to keep clean. Dust off the lids of your boxes, wipe down the shelves, and sweep the floor.

Step 4: Label It and Put It Away

Another trick that has helped with the organization of our garage (where I also keep all my extra office supplies, mailing supplies, etc.) is the map my daughter Kimber made of everything in our garage. It's amazing how much easier it is to find things now and avoid those search-and-destroy missions.

Step 5: Keep It Up

If you have a little more time to put into this project, here's an idea that will save you time in the end. I love the filing system the guys on *MythBusters* use for their storage shelves. They store things in similar-sized boxes and label each box with a white piece of paper on which they've printed in 200-point font general categories such as "Tubing" or "Explosives." This makes it easy to find things and to put them away.

I've done this in my garage. I slip the white piece of paper into a sheet protector and then tape it to the box. *Love it!*

Keeping the STEM Strong

Space

"Corral tools in a designated area and *always* put them back when finished," Carol says. "They tend to wander around aimlessly for days at a time when left on their own. Depending on how many tools you have, hang a pegboard on the wall for them, or buy or build a workbench for tool storage. If you already have a workbench in your garage but can't find it because it's piled high with other treasures, just dive in until you stumble upon it, clear it off, and then resolve to actually use it as a place for tools and storage. Buy a bucket with a compartmentalized skirt to hold a few household tools—convenient and portable!"

Time

"Store Christmas decorations in those cute red-and-green plastic containers so you can easily spot them and group them together," Carol says. "They usually go on sale near the holiday season. Keep them out of the everyday-use area."

Energy

If you have grown children and they've decided that their ice skates from seventh grade are too precious to get rid of (but not important enough to take with them to their new apartment), you can employ my strategy.

When Jeremy moved out, he did so in stages. First, his everyday stuff (clothes, sheets, and other necessities). Later, we helped him move his hockey equipment, which was taking up multiple shelves in the garage, and then his bike. Finally, we set a deadline for when the rest of his stuff needed to be out of the house or it was going on Freecycle. He picked up everything by midnight on the due date.

Money

Make sure you keep the area clear around the water heater and any other water-using appliances. In the case of leakage or machine malfunction, anything sitting around in cardboard boxes will be ruined. Plus, it makes the path for the repairman less hazardous. Yes, sadly, I am speaking with the voice of experience.

Bonus Projects

If you have a lot of boxes, consider this tip from Tonya:

"I use numbers on my boxes. I label the box with a huge 101, 102, 103 on the top, sides, and ends so no matter how I put it back, I can see it. Then on my computer, I keep a running list of what's in each box. Our small storage area is in what was once a detached garage, so I can look at the list ahead of time to find what box I'm looking for, and then easily find the box I need. I've moved to all clear boxes and don't store as much stuff, but this helps a lot with Christmas boxes or the last remaining hand-me-down clothes from the older brothers. Plus, I can add or delete when needed."—Tonya

Project Reports

"My husband and I were frustrated with the fact that our kids had moved out, but their stuff hadn't. We took your advice and gave them a deadline (with some additional enticement of homemade ravioli). Between our three kids, we were able to get rid of nineteen boxes. Some went to the kids' homes, and some things we happily took to the donation center for them. Our garage feels lighter!"—Terry

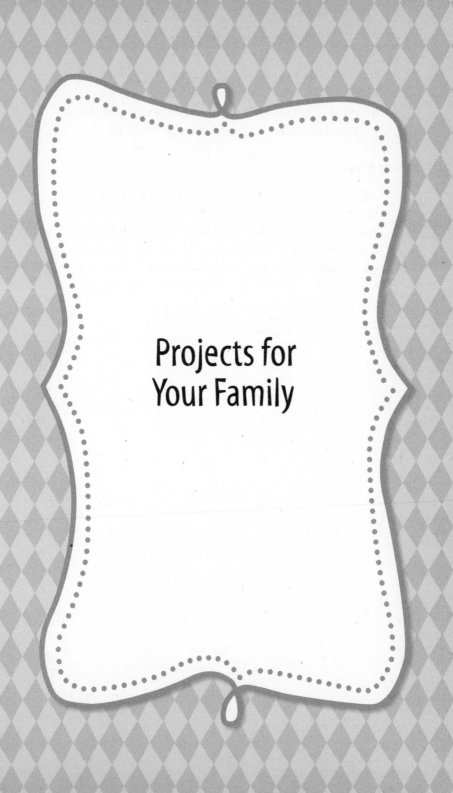

Projects for
Your Family

Project 8

Your Laundry

It had been a rough, stressful week, and I hadn't taken my own advice about doing laundry every day. Sadly, there was plenty of evidence of that sitting in our hallway. Hampers were overflowing, and my daughter was wearing her "ugly jeans." I was on a tight deadline, so Roger said, "Go. Write. I will take care of all the laundry today."

He had never been sexier than he was in that moment.

Roger spent the day washing, drying, folding, and putting away all those clean clothes. My hero! Later that night, as I was getting ready for bed, I put my dirty clothes in the hamper in our bedroom. Roger was crestfallen.

"But I was all caught up," he said.

Ah. Welcome to the world of laundry. Perhaps your experience with laundry is similar to my friend Jenny's: "Laundry makes me crazy! Also, the fact that I have a two-story house makes my situation with the laundry even crazier—nothing makes it upstairs. I think our laundry room has become the dressing room."

If you can relate, this project was written for you!

Step 1: Your Plan of Attack

In our house, our laundry system works for the most part. We all have clean clothes on a regular basis, and laundry just doesn't stress me out. If you have a system that works for you, great. Otherwise, here's what works in our house.

In our hall, we have four, 30-inch tall, plastic laundry hampers. Each one is for a different type of laundry:

- Whites
- Colored underwear
- Everyday clothes
- Jeans, towels, sweats

I also have a drawstring bag for shirts that I take to the cleaners and a garment bag for delicates. Both of those bags hang on the wall in the laundry area.

Everyone knows what basket their stuff needs to go in. If you want your clothes to be clean, then they need to go into the right laundry basket.

This system worked great except for a brief time when one of our boys didn't really care if he was wearing clean clothes. (I've heard several moms divulge this secret shame about their male offspring, so I knew it was just a phase. I'm here to report that both of our boys are contributing members of society and wear clean clothes every day.)

Other items I have found helpful to make the laundry space work:

- Two small laundry baskets for folding and putting away clothes
- Open storage tubs (about the size of shoe boxes)
- A hanger bar (we have a shower-curtain tension rod in our space)
- Hangers
- Hooks for hanging delicates
- A garbage sack for dryer lint and various oddities found in little boys' pockets

Step 2: Sort It Out

Now let's get your laundry area in order. Time for your three boxes and two bags. If your laundry area is small, you can tackle the whole thing in one project. If that feels overwhelming, then take just a section of the area (the tops of the washer and dryer, the shelves, the floor) and work on that. Take out only as much as you can put back in the time you've given yourself. (I suggest about fifteen minutes at a time.)

OTHER ROOMS

Place any dirty clothes that are sitting around in the appropriate hampers. Any clean clothes that are hanging out in that space need to be put away. Keep your regular laundry routine going as you're working on the space. Make sure that your laundry baskets are empty and ready for all the clean clothes you'll be folding and putting away.

PUT BACK

Hold on to this stuff for Step 3: Clean It Up.

GIVE AWAY

We have a permanent "Give Away" box in our laundry area for clothes our kids have outgrown and clothes we don't wear anymore. When the box gets full, I take it to Goodwill.

GARBAGE AND RECYCLING

Get rid of any old bottles of cleaner, laundry soap, etc. If you have bottles that have just a little bit left in them, either use those up first or combine the contents with bottles of the same product. Recycle whatever you can and throw the rest away.

Step 3: Clean It Up

Before you start stocking the shelves again, give them and your washer and dryer a good wipe down. You'll want many rags as this is one of the dustiest places in the house with all the blowout from the dryer (not to mention spilled laundry soap). This is also a good time to make an appointment to get your dryer vent cleaned, if needed.

Step 4: Label It and Put It Away

Shelving is important in this space. We have a couple of shelves above the washing machine and dryer. If that's not possible in your space, perhaps a small shelving unit would work.

This is also where those small open tubs come in. You can use anything from cute organizational boxes to cardboard shoeboxes. Just make sure that you won't mind if the boxes that hold liquid supplies get wet.

Take a minute and label each box with its contents. I have a labeler, but you could also use mailing labels or even "Hello, my name is…" labels. Make your font or printing giant so you have no trouble seeing which box is which. Here are some labels I have on my boxes:

- Stain removers
- Dryer sheets
- Socks
- Delicates bags

I also have room on my shelves for the laundry detergent, bleach, and fabric softener.

Step 5: Keep It Up

The best way to keep up on laundry is to do it every single day. Even if you are doing only your personal laundry, doing a load every or every other day will keep you from having to devote your whole Saturday to the chore.

The other thing that will make your life a lot easier is to remember this rule: *Until the clothes are put away, laundry isn't done.* Just because the clothes are clean and dry doesn't mean you've done laundry. Until those clothes are hung up in your closet or put away in your drawers, the laundry isn't done.

Just as I want you to start your day with an empty dishwasher, I want you to start your day with an empty washing machine, dryer, and two empty laundry baskets.

Are you one of those people who has no problem with the washing, drying, and folding of your clothes, but when it comes to putting all those clean clothes back in their rightful place, they never seem to make it? Please understand that you are not alone.

What's the main resistance to putting clothes away? Look inside your drawers and closets. Are they so stuffed it's hard to squeeze anything else in there? Well, no wonder you don't want to put your clothes away. Who would when finishing the task requires a crowbar?

I've experienced this with my kids as well. There's just about nothing on the planet that I hate more than to find a clean, folded shirt in the dirty clothes because some kid couldn't be bothered to put their clothes away (probably due to an overstuffed dresser or closet). It just lay on their bed or on their floor until it became part of the decomposing bottom layer. When they finally cleaned their room, the shirt was thrown back into the dirty clothes.

Grrrr. As far as I'm concerned, this is a capital offense punishable by the removal of all forms of communication (TV, iPod, Internet, tin cans and string).

This is one of those problems where you have to work backward. Getting rid of all the clothes that you and your kids don't wear is one of the simplest ways to stay on top of laundry. I know it doesn't seem like it will, but just try it.

Keeping the STEM Strong

Space

I can't say it enough—the fewer clothes you have to deal with, the easier laundry is going to be. Even though I live where the weather varies between nice and gorgeous, I still swap out about 30 percent of my wardrobe every winter and summer. But beware. Store only those things that you love and will wear again when the seasons change.

Time

The main time-waster with laundry is searching for clothes in piles.

Remember, laundry isn't done for the day until it's all put away and the laundry baskets (not hampers) are empty.

Energy

KIDS AND LAUNDRY

The best way to save energy with laundry is to have someone else do it. Since only three of us are now living at home, I find it easier to do all of our wash together. However, when the kids were younger and everyone was living at home, each child had a day to get two loads of laundry through the whole process (wash, dry, fold, put away).

Many of my friends have decided to let each of their kids do their laundry in one load so there's no sorting, and each child is responsible for their own clothes.

You may want to grab all the white socks, underwear, and shirts every once in a while to run a bleach load to keep them looking bright, but for the most part, your kids' clothes will be just fine going through the laundry in one big load.

> "My kids (twelve, ten, and eight) have been doing household laundry as a chore for a while now, but after hearing about the idea of not sorting colors, I've given them a hamper in their rooms and they're now responsible just for their own laundry. If they run out of something clean, they have no one else to blame. Love it! Of course I still have to be careful of new items that may bleed, and I still do the regular household laundry (sheets, towels). But this sure cuts down on my load."—Vikki

Whether your kids do their laundry on their own or as part of the household laundry is up to you. It is critical, however, that all of your kids know how to do laundry and participate.

DON'T LET IT SIT

The biggest time and energy waster with laundry is clothes that sit in the washer, dryer, or laundry basket. Clothes that sit in the washer start to smell sour and have to be washed again. Clothes that sit in the dryer or hamper become a wrinkled mess, and aren't we all tempted to throw them through the wash again?

UNMATCHED SOCKS

I believe that unmatched socks are a spiritual drain of energy. If your unmatched socks have gone to your laundry area to die, now is the time to make some decisions. Here is my sock plan:

1. Gather all the unmatched socks you can find. Take them to a happy place such as in front of the TV and put on a girly movie. Or perhaps play Beyonce's "Single Ladies (Put a Ring on It)" while matching up all those single socks.

2. Sort your socks into four different piles:

   • Long white socks

   • Long colored socks

   • Short white socks

   • Short colored socks

3. Match each and every sock you can find a mate to.

4. Put the remaining socks in a bag and label it with the style and date (Long Colored Socks—April).

5. Have a spot in the laundry area for a mismatched sock bin. Make sure it has an open top so it's easy to fling socks into.

6. Over the next month, encourage your family to put every unmatched sock in their rooms, gym bags, under their beds into the laundry. Over the next month, those socks that are mismatched will end up in the mismatched socks bin.

7. After about a month, go through all the socks, repeating the system described above. Whatever socks still don't have a match get recycled.

It may seem harsh to pitch all those unmatched socks, but there's no sense paying rent on clothes that no one is wearing.

And here's one more super sock tip:

> "Until my twins were five years old, I washed all their socks in a delicates bag. You don't lose socks that way, and more importantly, your husband doesn't have a small pink sock fall out of his pant leg as he walks to a business meeting with his boss."—Christy

Money

STAIN REMOVAL

My sister-in-law has a reputation for being able to get a stain out of any garment. My niece Elsa is a toddler, so Lucinda is getting a lot of practice these days. Here is Lucinda's surefire stain-removal strategy:

1. Spray with stain remover.

2. Rub and let set for a while.

3. Put the garment in a bucket of OxiClean mixed with water (one-quarter cup of OxiClean per one to two gallons of water) and let soak until your next load of clothes. (Sometimes I have more than one bucket of garments soaking at a time because I like to separate anything that might bleed in the wash.)

Check the stained items before transferring them to the dryer. If the stain is still visible, put the garment aside and start the process over again (though the stains often come out even after going through the dryer). If a white or light garment still has a faint stain, dry it outside as sun exposure helps lighten stains.

Bonus Projects

I think your laundry area should be a place you want to spend time (or at least don't dread). In my past homes, we've hung up kids' artwork and cartoons on tiny clotheslines. Now that my space is superlimited, I have some whimsical, bright-colored hooks that look like the tail end of a dog. I also have an iPod stand in there so I can listen to music or books while doing the laundry.

You could even hang pictures of the people you're folding laundry for and some verses about serving. Figure out what will bless you in that space.

Project Reports

> "We have found that the collapsible or pop-up hampers are wonderful space savers. We do a similar laundry system as the one you describe. Each child has his or her own hamper, so when I do laundry, everything in any given load belongs to just one child. The bathroom has a clothing hamper and a towel hamper, so those are sorted as the kids take off their clothes or dump their towels. The collapsible hampers fold up flat, so as I'm washing or drying each load, I can tuck the hamper alongside the washer or dryer and it doesn't take up precious real estate."—Sharon

Project 9

Your Family's Schedule

When my friend Vicki's young grandchildren complain sometimes that they're bored, she reminds them, "Bored? Christians don't ever have to be bored. There's always something we can do for the Lord! You can bake cookies for a neighbor, draw a picture, write a letter, or visit someone who's lonely. Pray and see what God wants you to do, and then I'll help you get started."

Your Plan of Attack

Given the uniqueness of this project, I won't follow the five-step outline I've used for the previous projects. But I hope you'll find the following scheduling ideas equally helpful in your efforts to get yourself organized.

WHAT YOU'LL NEED

Write on a calendar all your family's activities so you know where your commitments are. To make this calendar as helpful and easy to use as possible, I suggest the following:

- A monthly calendar with large boxes for each day
- A pen attached to the calendar so you never have to go looking
- A highlighter to draw attention to important appointments you don't want your husband or the kids to forget

(Not that they'll check the calendar, but you're more likely
to see it and remind them if it's highlighted.)

WHAT TO DO

Get everything on the calendar. And I do mean everything. Write
it down even if you have standing appointments every week, even if
you know your schedule by heart. Put it down.

For some reason, you have a mental edge over your schedule when
you write everything down and see in black and white (or green and
white if you're that kind of girl) what you have going on.

It's critical, at some point in this process, to confer with the other
members of your household and get their schedules as well. This way,
you know when your teen needs to borrow the car, when you need
to get the morning off to drive for the field trip, and what night your
sushi-hating husband will be serving at church and you can have California rolls for dinner.

The family schedule is less about a plan of attack and more about
making sure you don't overcommit while out in the world, and then
try to cram it all into your life when you get home.

Here are some ideas to consider if you are living out of your minivan:

UNDERSTAND YOUR CHILD'S NEED FOR SPEED (OR NEUTRAL)

Justen and Kimberly come from the same parents, but they could
not be more different. Kimber has boundless energy and will insti-
gate activities with friends. She was involved in a staggering number
of activities in high school, and while she likes her downtime, she will
take a variety of forms of public transportation to be with her peeps.
Justen's energy is decidedly different. If I had to pick a motto for him
it would be, "Why stand when you can sit? Why sit when you can lie
down?"

My friend Robin has struggled with, and now has some victory over,
the family schedule. I asked her what her biggest struggle was with her
kids' time, and I love her totally raw answer:

"Even though I have declared war on our busy culture, I still fall into the trap of wanting my family to look like everyone else's in some ways: busy athletic kids, piles of dirty uniforms, and balls falling out of my car when I open the tailgate. What I do have are two kids who aren't particularly interested in sports, at least in a traditional 'team sport with a uniform and a trophy' kind of way."

Don't we all fall into that trap at one time or another? So much of managing our kids' schedules is knowing who they are, knowing who we are as a family, and then deciding with God's help how to manage all of our time and energy.

I love Robin's advice and have sprinkled her thoughts throughout this project, such as this reminder on the place of prayer: "God is the one responsible for creating the child, and he knows their needs best. As you pray, he will be faithful to reveal to you what your child needs."

My son is an introvert, so after he went to Scout camp for a week and then stayed with friends for three days while his dad and I were on a trip, I cleared his calendar for the rest of the week so he could recharge. On the flip side, I have a friend whose son I've compared to a Labrador puppy. He craves constant stimulation. If she can survive his puppyhood, the rest will be great! He is active and benefits greatly from multiple activities that keep his fun productive and safe.

I have another friend with a child who drove her bonkers. He was always late and a slow mover. There was nothing wrong with him; he just didn't crave moving through life at light speed as she did. She could either learn to be sensitive to his needs and find a balance between them or look forward to tons of unnecessary conflict.

Philippians 2:3-4 provides good guidance to follow: "Do nothing out of selfish ambition or vain conceit. Rather, in humility value others above yourselves, not looking to your own interests but each of you to the interests of the others."

Finally, when you're taking a look at your family's overall schedule, think about these wise words from mentor Kathy Box: "What your kids really need is time with their parents and not necessarily another activity where you sit a hundred feet away and clap for them."

Keeping the STEM Strong

Space

While we want to keep space in our kids' lives (and in ours), too much space can be detrimental for some kids. Pastor Danny Box says, "If you're not scared, you're not growing." This can include trusting God to stretch us when it might be easier and safer to sit on the couch. Space is important, but so is stretching.

Time

> "At the beginning of the year I ask someone from the church office to send me the master calendar for the year. That way youth events, women's retreats, and ministry commitments can keep priority even when the official announcement is much closer to the event. Right when the sports calendar or school-year calendar gets released, I write down every holiday, early release, or other important date so it's already there when I'm trying to add other things in later."—Robin

Energy

PUTTING LIMITS ON THEIR COMMITMENTS

Naomi Williams shares with us how she lets each of her kids, especially her teenagers, pick three activities at a time:

> "*Game*—something fun for them to enjoy, such as a sport, music, or robotics; something they find fun wherever their passions are strong.
>
> *Grow*—a time to grow in their faith through Bible study, discipleship group, or youth group, whichever is a better fit for your child's personality.

Give—a place to serve others. The world calls it volunteering; God calls it serving. Have them pray about where God would lead them to grow by humbly serving others."

Money

My friend Miranda and her husband had a budget for each kid's activities per year. The kids had to help decide how to spend the money. One year their daughter wanted new kneepads for soccer, but if she chose to spend her money there, she risked not having enough to go on her band trip the following month. Their daughter decided that using her pads from the previous year would suffice.

Bonus Projects

If you're going to get serious about a family schedule, spend the extra twenty dollars to get a calendar that will work.

Calendar resources. The "More Time Moms Family Organizer" is a great calendar a friend recommended years ago that I still use faithfully. It has a cute cartoon banner across the top, and the spaces are large enough that I eliminated the day planner years ago. Because it's a sixteen-month calendar, I can start in September if I want. You can order online at www.moretimemoms.com. FlyLady also has a great calendar, the "I'm FLYing Calendar," with lots of room to write. It's available online at www.flylady.net. Both of these calendars are under twenty dollars (not including shipping).

Project Reports

"Every time I check my e-mail I bring my calendar with me. As I read my e-mails, I write future events down on the calendar. It saves me from spending hours trying to go back and find that event that I thought vaguely was happening soon."—Robin

Meal Planning

When it comes to saving time, money, and energy, there's no area more critical than meal planning. By doing a little planning at the beginning of the month, you will reap a ton of benefits for weeks, including:

- Less hectic evenings
- Less money spent eating out
- More time connecting with friends and family at the dinner table
- Better, fresher foods

For a full-kitchen approach to meal planning and prep, check out my book *The "What's for Dinner?" Solution.* But for a head start, here are a few tips and ideas to get you cooking.

Step 1: Your Plan of Attack

I want you to create a master calendar of meals for a month. Here's what you'll need as you sit down and make your plans:

- *Blank calendar.* Go to www.ProjectsForYourSoul.com for a printable blank calendar.
- *Pens*
- *Your family calendar*
- *Recipe binder*

Step 2: Sort It Out

Look at the activities and schedules of those you're cooking for. Most households develop a weekly rhythm over time. Tuesdays and Thursdays tend to be less chaotic around our house, while Mondays, everyone seems to work, and Wednesdays have always been a church night. Fridays are usually just Roger and me for dinner, and our big family dinners (when even the kids who don't live at home come back) are on Sunday evenings. While this schedule can vary wildly (especially when I'm traveling), it does have a basic flow that helps me plan our meals.

Step 3: Label It

Once you have an idea of the schedule, label each night with the kind of meal you need to have. If you need to have dinner ready when you get home (and not worry about it burning in the oven), then a slow-cooker recipe could be the ticket for you. If one of your kids will be home in the afternoon and you won't be, how about a freezer meal?

Here are some of my meal categories that I use for planning:

FREEZER MEALS

I prepare these meals ahead of time and stick them in the freezer to be pulled out and cooked (or reheated) at a later date. When my kids were younger, we did many casseroles this way. Now it tends to be marinated pork roasts, chicken breasts, soups, and stews.

SLOW-COOKER MEALS

I put the ingredients in the pot in the morning, and dinner is ready for me when I get home. It's a miracle each and every time. This is especially great for nights when all your teens are coming home at different hours. Just set the slow cooker to low to keep things warm.

LOOP MEALS

LOOP (LeftOvers On Purpose) is a great way to cook once and eat twice. We generally eat our biggest meal on Sundays when the whole family is over. If Roger is going to barbeque steaks on Sunday, I'll ask him to throw a couple more on the grill for us to slice up and put on top of salads on Tuesday night. Cook once, eat twice. Beautiful.

Fast Food at Home

You can do these quick meals on the fly. Pita pizza, chicken salad, pasta and sauce are all things that don't take a lot of advance planning but are still yummy.

Every Man for Himself

That's what we've called our "clean out the fridge" nights. I just heard a new term for it: YOYO (You're On Your Own) Nights. Love it.

By following the above schedule, this is how one of our weekly menus would go:

> **Sunday:** The whole family is over—LeftOvers On Purpose, Round 1
> *Menu:* Spice-rubbed pork roast with potatoes and ratatouille
>
> **Monday:** Everyone works or is on a different schedule— Slow-Cooker Meal
> *Menu:* Vegetable soup with bread-machine whole wheat bread
>
> **Tuesday:** Everyone's home—LeftOvers On Purpose, Round 2
> *Menu:* Leftover sliced pork (from Sunday) with homemade mac-n-cheese and asparagus
>
> **Wednesday:** Mom's home late—Freezer Meal
> *Menu:* Poppyseed chicken, bagged salad, and baked cinnamon apples
>
> **Thursday:** Everyone's home—Fast Food at Home
> *Menu:* Veggie pita pizzas with turkey pepperoni
>
> **Friday:** It's usually just Roger and me—Every Man for Himself (or YOYO)

Saturday: Everyone's home—Freezer Meal
Menu: Teriyaki chicken with rice and grilled veggie kabobs

Besides your schedule, here are some other things to consider when making up your menus.

Time of year. I like to eat seasonally as much as possible. If my garden is bursting with squash, or the last time I went to the market the strawberries looked anemic and were from a foreign country, those things can influence my meal planning.

What I already have on hand. When I hit a great sale on chicken, I can stock up freezer-style. But when I'm heading out to the farmers' market, those super-fresh fruits and veggies have an expiration date. I want to be thoughtful with the food I purchase and use it before I lose it, whenever possible. So many times I have bought what I already had on hand because I didn't check before making my meal plan and heading to the store.

Is the weather okay? This may not be the biggest consideration, but last year I put together a month's worth of meals for June without thinking once about barbecuing. Why have beef stew in the summer or Asian chicken salad in the dead of winter? Celebrate the seasons with delicious food.

Step 4: Keep It Up

Once you have a master calendar of the types of meals you plan to eat for a month, go ahead and make copies of it for the next couple of months. Yes, schedules change, but when you have a template to work from, it makes life a whole lot easier. Just make sure that you give yourself some flexibility so that you're not locked into a schedule when you have to work late or your daughter made it to the state soccer finals.

Having a plan where you need to make adjustments for one or two nights is a whole lot better than no plan and panic-driven trips through a drive-thru.

Keeping the STEM Strong

Space

If recipe books are overtaking your kitchen, photocopy your favorite recipes for your personal use and put them in a binder. Then donate the books to your favorite charity and get your kitchen back.

INGREDIENTS

For your first couple of months of planning, don't try out recipes with exotic ingredients you don't have on hand. Nothing is worse than buying a Costco-sized container of curry spice only to realize someone in your family will "never eat anything with curry ever again for the rest of my life."

USE-IT-UP COOKING

One of the best ways to plan meals is to see what's hiding out in your cabinets and freezer and use those things first. It's amazing the collection of great food I already have in my house and don't use simply because it's not in the front of the freezer.

Time

Give yourself some space to plan—don't try to do the planning, shopping, and cooking all in the same day. Give yourself a week to do the planning, shopping, and a little advance cooking for the freezer or LOOP meals.

Energy

You may be one of those lucky people who has the opportunity to share the meal planning with someone else. If that's the case, I suggest for your first time planning that you set aside a good hour or so to go through the exercise. It actually is a lot of fun to do this with another person.

Money

"Our health-food store has good prices on bulk items, including spices. Those five-dollar poppy seeds from the grocery store cost under two dollars in bulk. This gives a way to try some new spices without investing a lot of money. I buy my sea salt there for thirty-seven cents a pound. Not everything is a deal, but if you know your prices, it can be. If I need a specialty flour or rice, I have found shopping there to be much cheaper."—Tonya

Bonus Projects

If you've spent some time organizing your menu and have an idea what you're going to eat for the month (or even the week), you're going to save a lot of money by not resorting to desperation. May I suggest you go to the library and check out a cookbook with some new recipes and inspiration?

Project 11

Grocery Shopping

I wish I could say it had never happened to me.

You know, you're running to the store to pick up the oranges for the orange-cranberry scones you promised to bring to your next-door neighbor's house for your monthly Bunco night. On your way to the store, you remember that you're out of milk for your coffee (and had to explain to your four-year-old that it was way more important for Mommy to have milk with her coffee than for him to have milk with his cereal and wouldn't it be fun to eat his cornflakes with apple juice?), and you really need to grab a bag of kitty litter before Muffins stages a protest…oh and you have a coupon for the kind of cereal your husband likes.

So you get home an hour later, $127.53 poorer, with no oranges and find the cereal coupon stuck to the front of your fridge.

Don't let this be the weekly drama that gets played out in your house. Shop with a list, shop with a plan.

Step 1: Your Plan of Attack

Download the shopping lists from my website www.ProjectsFor YourSoul.com. These can help you to create your own list as you take an inventory of what you have and what you need.

Be sure to divide your areas. If you have a refrigerator, large freezer, food cabinets, and a pantry, just take one area at a time. And the time will fly much faster if you're listening to a great book or some amazing music on your iPod.

Instead of the three boxes and two bags, I want you to have your counter cleared, both your dishwasher and sink empty, and your garbage and recycling bins empty.

I also want you to grab a package of stickers. I don't care what kind of sticker—use up your kids' Snoopy stickers, use some colored dots, whatever. I'll tell you more about the stickers in a moment. Also, grab a yellow highlighter.

Step 2: Sort It Out

First, I want you to clean out your food areas.

Refrigerator

I know I should clean out my fridge once a week, but honestly, when I'm at my busiest, one of the following three events has to happen before I dig in:

1. I detect an untraceable smell.

2. The take-out containers make it impossible for me to find a place to put my pint of nonfat milk. (You don't get to judge until you have five adults living under one roof.)

3. I'm getting ready to go to my local warehouse store.

Items I will be taking a long hard look at in the fridge are:

- All the ketchups, designer mustards, pineapple salsas, and similar items that have ended up in my condiment graveyard

- Any take-out boxes (This may sever some relationships kid-wise, but I'm willing to run the risk.)

- The veggie bin (I get motivated to eat healthy when I'm in the store and at the farmers' market, but when it comes to preparing those super-healthy-organic-and-locally-grown veggies…their chances of making it into actual dishes are about fifty-fifty.)

- Milk (All milks will be given the sniff test.)

Cupboards and Pantry Areas

Look for boxed and canned food that is past its "best by" date. For both boxed and canned food, I mark the expiration date with a highlighter.

Freezer

If you can't identify it, pitch it. If you don't know what decade it made it into the deep freeze, pitch it.

PUT BACK

Hold off on putting things back until you've given the area a good cleaning.

GIVE AWAY

You should hold no guilt for getting rid of food that you're not going to eat. One option is to donate it, along with some of the food that you do eat regularly, to a food pantry. Here is my local food bank's general list of most-needed items.

The Food Bank needs nutritious, nonperishable foods:

- Meals in a can (stew, chili, soup)
- Tuna and canned meat
- Peanut butter
- Canned foods with pop-top lids
- Low-sugar cereals
- Canned fruit packed in juice
- Canned vegetables (low salt)

The Food Bank also needs nutritious, nonperishable, single-serving foods for use in programs for children:

- Pop-top tuna
- 100-percent fruit rolls
- Raisins
- Graham crackers
- Unsweetened applesauce
- Cheese and crackers
- Fruit cups
- Low-sugar cereal bowls
- Pretzels
- 100-percent fruit juice boxes
- Granola bars (without peanuts)

Some food banks ask that you not donate items packaged in glass or bulk quantities of rice, flour, and sugar. They do not have the resources to repackage and distribute those.

So when you want to donate those unopened cans of sardines your dad left during Thanksgiving, be sure to toss in some canned peaches as well. Oh, and if you find any money stashed in your pantry, they will gladly accept that as well.

GARBAGE AND RECYCLING

This is why I wanted your dishwasher emptied. Dispose of any food that has gone bad and start recycling all those containers. If you haven't done this for a while, don't freak out at the number of things that might be lurking there. It happens to everyone. (OK, not to type-A clean freaks, but they never have the fun of playing the refrigerator game, "Guess what that used to be?")

Step 3: Clean It Up

Wipe all the surface areas down. I like to remove the shelves in my fridge and soak them in the sink to get them extra clean.

Step 4: Label It and Put It Away

Just as in any other area of your home, you should know what goes in your fridge and cabinets, and where. I have labels in my cabinet and even labels inside my fridge for where things should go.

One of the smartest things I did in the fridge was to get a few plastic bins to group like items together: All the salad dressings go in one, all the cheeses go in another, and condiments for sandwiches (mayo, mustard, pickles, ketchup) in another. I can take the whole salad-dressing basket to the dinner table and everyone can grab their favorite.

When you find perfectly good food in your fridge or cupboards, but there's an expiration date looming large, put one of those stickers on the package. This has worked wonders in our household! When I see that sticker, I know it's a "use it or lose it" situation, and I work hard to figure out fun recipes for that package of chicken garlic sausage. You can also use blue painters tape for this. Just slap a piece of blue tape on anything that needs it. Blue tape is great for sealing up opened packages as well.

Step 5: Keep It Up

Take a Big Inventory

I do this about once a year, usually before a big cooking day. I go through the pantry, cupboards, freezer, and fridge and take stock of what I already have. This is also an excellent time to closely scrutinize all the "best by" dates on my foods, use up the ones that are close to expiring, and pitch the ones that are past their prime.

I have included inventory sheets on our website (www.ProjectsFor YourSoul.com) for you to download. Feel free to customize these to fit your kitchen's needs. Just because I listed something on the inventory sheets doesn't mean you need that item; these are just common grocery items for most families. I've also included space for you to write in your family's favorites.

Here are the areas I want you to inventory:

- Freezer

- Refrigerator
- Pantry
- Cupboards
- Spices

Once you know what you have, it will be much easier to know what you need.

MAKE YOUR LISTS

I shop a couple of different places, so I have a couple of different lists.

Warehouse store. This is where I do most of my bulk shopping:

- Frozen chicken breasts
- Whole roasted chickens
- Ground beef
- Pork roasts
- Pork chops
- Marinades
- Cheese
- Pasta
- Rice
- Canned veggies (especially tomatoes)
- Oatmeal
- Spices (only ones we use regularly)
- Vanilla (I use vanilla in mass quantities, and it's drastically cheaper at a warehouse store.)
- Coffee
- Cereal
- Crackers

- Extra-virgin olive oil
- Butter
- Flour (since we bake a lot of our own breads)
- Popcorn
- Sugar for baking
- Honey

Regular grocery store:

- Produce (We stopped buying most produce at warehouse stores once we joined a veggie co-op. However, when we want something specific, we buy it at the grocery store in order to get the quantity we need instead of the quantity we and our six neighbors would use if we bought it at a warehouse store.)
- Eggs
- Milk
- Meats that I don't want to purchase in jumbo packs (sausage, for example)
- Breads

Now let's be clear. Like you, I don't purchase all of these things every trip. When we had more kids living at home, we bought eggs and milk at the warehouse store. However, it's good to develop some guidelines for where you purchase what. We hit the warehouse store only about once a month these days, and since we have a tiny fridge, that dictates what we buy.

Keeping the STEM Strong

Space

Divide bulk purchases with a friend. You may not need ten pounds of potatoes, but five would be great.

Time and Energy

If you and a friend both like the same specialty store, how about taking turns shopping? This is a great idea, especially if you have young kids. (One person babysits; the other person shops.)

Money

For every ten minutes I spend planning my shopping trip and making a list, I save about ten dollars. Advance planning keeps me from repeating purchases or buying perishables I already have, and it helps me think creatively about the food we have on hand that needs to be used up.

For especially lean weeks, I will challenge myself to use up those packages of leftover frozen turkey hanging out in the freezer or trying new recipes with the canned foods I have in my pantry. I'm grateful for the months when I can stock up on great sales so that in the months when I want to be more careful with our grocery budget, I have back stock to pull from.

PLAN BACKWARD

One of the best strategies for cooking is to look at what you already have and plan your meals around those items. There's no sense buying chicken thighs for a recipe when you have a bunch of frozen drumsticks lurking in the back of the freezer. Besides, meat starts to lose its flavor or can suffer from freezer burn if it's on ice for months.

So look at your list and see what you already have. Since meat is generally the most expensive part of the meal, use those items first. Then look through your favorite cookbooks to plan your meals around the ingredients you have on hand.

When looking for recipes, look for ones that don't require a bunch of exotic ingredients and are simple to prepare. There's nothing worse than buying a tiny jar of poppy seeds for a "cheap" recipe only to discover that poppy seeds are anything but cheap. Use ingredients you're familiar with, and then allow yourself to experiment occasionally with one or two dishes that require a small number of unusual ingredients. If you don't like those ingredients, pitch them or give them to someone who will use them. There's no sense keeping that jar of chili paste you hated if you're never going to use it again.

CHECK THE SALES

Each Monday the sales flyers from my favorite grocery stores show up in my mailbox. I find out what the loss leaders are and see what meals I can create around those. If something is on a particularly good sale, I'll stock up only if it will keep well, even if I'm not planning to use it right away. This is "shopping for my pantry," replenishing items that I like to have on hand or can get at a great price.

Bonus Projects

Spend some time creating a master shopping list on a spreadsheet, such as Excel, for all the grocery items you buy.

To create your list, save up your grocery receipts for a month and see everything that you've purchased. This is a great way to know what you are actually buying. Put all of those items (along with anything else you know you might buy) onto your shopping list. That way, the next time you go to the store, all you have to do is make checkmarks beside those items you need.

I've divided my master list into three sections: Grocery Store, Warehouse Store, and Other. I can print off that list, take a quick inventory, and see what I have on hand. That way I don't spend extra time or money purchasing grocery items I don't need for the month.

Project 12

Kids' Chores

It's just easier to do it myself.

Ugh. How many times have I thought that? Chores felt like more of a chore to me than they did to the kids. There was often slacking, lacking, and outright defying when it came to chores. However, I persisted. You see, I had two main goals when it came to chores and kids in my house:

1. I wanted help around the house. I know this seems obvious, but with three teens living in our house at the same time, it wasn't a luxury, it was a necessity. Also, with working from home but often traveling, if I didn't have help, people didn't eat.

2. When my boys get married, I want my daughters-in-law to rise up and call me blessed. There was no way that I was going to let loose on the world men who couldn't do their own laundry, cook for themselves, or do their own dishes.

Even though so many times it felt like a lost cause, I persisted when it came to chores.

Corporate Training

The best companies take time away from productivity to train employees—it's a short-term sacrifice for long-term gain. I thought it was obvious how to load a dishwasher or how to fold clothes, but I made the huge mistake of not training the kids, and then being frustrated when their efforts didn't meet my (unreasonable) expectations.

Because of some special challenges in our family (blending a family, kids with some learning challenges), we went back and forth on how to divvy up the chores. Finally, what worked for us was to come up with a list that each kid was responsible for every day for a week. Here are some typical lists:

Kimberly

- Help mom get dinner ready at 5:30
- Water backyard plants
- Fluff pillows and blankets and straighten up living room in the morning
- Ask Mom

Justen

- Afternoon dishes
- Garbage and recycling
- Wipe down the counters and appliances
- Ask Mom

Jeremy

- Evening dishes
- Sweep and mop kitchen
- Fold and put away dryer basket
- Ask Dad

Each kid had an "ask Mom/ask Dad" on his or her chore list depending on who the bio parent was. This way, when we saw something that needed attention (the cat box needed a *big* cleaning, the downstairs bathroom needed a once-over), we could have one of them take care of it.

In addition to those daily chores, each kid was required to give us one hour of work on Saturday for anything we needed done around the house.

Keeping the STEM Strong

Space

I was amazed that when the kids started doing chores, they were a little more careful about where their stuff was. I didn't find nearly as much stuff lying around when they knew, eventually, they'd have to be the ones picking it up.

Time

> "Make a chart to track who's responsible for specific chores and the completion time for each chore. Depending on the ages of your children, make it a fun game with stickers they can place on a chart to see their success. No matter what the ages of family members, however, be sure to offer them your appreciation for their contributions to the family chores."—Carol

Energy

As your kids get older, so should the scope of their responsibilities. One way to gauge when responsibilities should increase is to ask yourself, Is my load getting heavier or lighter? I needed to realize that every time my kids were given new privileges (using the car, staying out later, more freedom with how they spend their time), their responsibilities needed to increase as well (getting the tank filled up with gas, taking the car to get washed, doing the dishes), even if they were getting home late.

Money

I won't get into a discussion of being paid for chores here, but Roger and I always had ways for our kids to earn money around the house. Some chores are done because you live in the house and we all pitch in, but some extra chores were of the work-equals-pay variety.

For my daughter, Kimber, this was a great way for her to support her friend habit without having to give up her afterschool activities.

Bonus Projects

Make a master list of all the chores that need to be done around the house. If a kid wants extra money, you can always have a list of things they can do to earn that money.

Project 13

Paperwork

Paperwork. Is there any word that more frequently causes us to groan internally than the word *paperwork*? Ugh.

When computers made their appearance, we were all teased with the idea of the "paperless society." What it really meant was that anyone with a computer and a printer could cheaply churn out even more paperwork that I now have to deal with.

But I want to give you hope. You don't have to be overrun, overwhelmed, or feel as though you are in over your head anymore. I have a simple system that has turned me from someone who paid my bills late, forgot about dentist appointments, and lost receipts, to the woman who can find most things most of the time. (Hey, I didn't say I had a magic wand.)

Step 1: Your Plan of Attack

I strongly suggest you gather all your loose paper into one place—every mail pile in your living room, all those magazines you want to save but aren't sure why, the random sticky notes, coupons, envelopes. Search every nook and cranny around your house, and everything that was once a tree (except for your furniture) goes in the box.

If you're dealing with more than one box of papers, perhaps you should limit yourself to fifteen minutes of sorting at a time so as not to become overwhelmed. (I know that large stacks of paper make me want to roll up in a ball in a corner and weep uncontrollably.)

Step 2: Sort It Out

Keep up with your three boxes, but I hope for this project you'll need only one bag because you can recycle paper in your community. You'll also want an extra box—a "Life Organization File (LOF)" box. More on that soon.

OTHER ROOMS

Sometimes you need to move papers to other places—perhaps an order form needs to be put in your son's backpack, or you have something that needs to be mailed right away. Maybe you need your husband to look over an invitation, or directions to tomorrow's board meeting need to go into your purse. Great, put those in this box and make some time to get all the paperwork where it needs to be.

PUT BACK

This box is for anything that you need to file. Every household should have a simple filing system for receipts, warranties, tax returns, and all those other papers that aren't currently "in motion" but may need to be referred to at a later date.

Try to keep your files as lean and mean as possible. You don't need to keep your check stubs from college or warranties from a fridge you no longer own. Since so much of our lives are stored on our computers, we can get rid of a lot of the paperwork we no longer need. You can find most instruction manuals online, scan articles to keep on your computer, and put reminders directly on your digital calendar.

If you have extensive files, I suggest a great book to you. *Getting Things Done* by David Allen has a no-nonsense plan for keeping your files usable.

Examine whether you need more than one drawer of file storage. Perhaps if you work at home or if you have a spouse who loves doing the bills and keeps everything, fine. If it's working for you, great. If it's not, try getting rid of most of your paper.

Create for yourself a Life Organization File box. This box is for any papers that are currently in play. In this box, place the stuff like tickets to the theater and insurance paperwork that needs to be mailed. In just a bit, I'm going to tell you what to do with all that paper.

GIVE AWAY

Do you have magazines that your library or some other organization would love? Ask first, and then drop them off.

GARBAGE AND RECYCLING

You shouldn't have much for the garbage, but I suggest a shredder for any sensitive information you want to get rid of.

Step 3: Clean It Up

Whatever area you just gathered up your paperwork from, can I make a suggestion? Give it a good cleaning, and then put something beautiful there. If you just uncovered your kitchen counter from a pile of papers, don't leave that space blank—put a beautiful bowl, a vase, a basket of fruit, something there so that you will be reminded to never pile up those papers again.

Step 4: Label It and Put It Away

Papers you need to retrieve later go in the file drawer. Papers you still need to work on go into your Life Organization File.

THE LIFE ORGANIZATION FILE

If you're anything like me, you have a million "notes to self," and every once in a while a little piece of paper can get lost in your shuffle. I have found a very simple system that can help even the most hopelessly unorganized person amaze her friends and family with clever holiday ideas and on-time birthday greetings (as well as getting the bills paid on time). Here are the items you'll need, most of which you probably have on hand:

- One file box

- Twelve hanging files with tabs
- Thirty-one file folders
- One permanent marker
- Sticky notes
- Your home calendar
- Your home address book
- A book of stamps

Putting Your Life Organization File Together

1. On each of the tabs of the twelve hanging files write one of the months of the year (January–December) and on each of the file folders, the days of the month (1–31).

2. Put all the month files in the back of your file box, and the 1–31 folders in the front.

Using Your Life Organization File

Once your file is put together, the hardest part is over. Now all you have to do is use it.

For Everyday Life

1. Set aside some time at the beginning of your week to file the paperwork that needs it. I do paperwork on Mondays, so any bills, information the kids bring home from school, sales flyers, coupons, etc. that show up the week before go into the coming Monday's file folder. Say that Monday is the 14th. I have a sticky note that I put on folder 14 to remind me that's where I'll put all the papers I will be filing on that day.

2. Monday the 14th I go through all those papers, work on them or file them, and then move the sticky note to folder 21—the next Monday when I will be doing paperwork.

Here are some examples of things I do with those little slips of paper:

- Make a list of errands
- See what sales are coming up
- Note bills that need to be paid (or filed for later)
- Jot down things I need to put on the calendar

I check to see if I can (or must) take care of any of these items immediately. When I open my mail, I always do it with my recycle basket, calendar, and Life Organization File (LOF) right next to me. Dates get entered on the calendar, papers are recycled, and forms, bills, and important paperwork are dropped into the LOF.

So, say you have a pile of papers just sitting on your desk. Here is how I would go through that pile with my LOF:

- *Bills*—Put these in the coming Monday's file.

- *Invitation to a party two months away on October 10*—Put that in the October file. When you get to October, you will put everything in that file into the numbered file folders.

- *Sales flyers*—Put those in next Monday's file so you can create your shopping list based on what's on sale.

Some Additional Tips

- You know how you come across a great recipe for Christmas cookies on January 15? Clip out that recipe and drop it in your December file. It will be waiting for you next holiday season.

- Find the perfect Maxine card for your sister, but her birthday is still months away? Buy it now (saving you an emergency trip to the store) and place it in her birthday month's file.

- See a great article on the Internet on flowerpot painting and want to try it out when you visit your mom in May? Just drop it in the May file, and you'll remember to take it with you.

- Once a year I go on a greeting-card buying spree. I buy cards that are just right for the people in my life, and some general ones to have on hand. Dayspring.com is a great resource for general cards. When I get the cards home, I address them and stamp the envelopes, but do not sign them until I'm ready to mail them. I want my greetings to be fresh and interesting.

- This filing system also makes a great gift for an older family member who likes to send cards. Show them your file first to see if it's something they would use. Some of my relatives in their nineties have better memories than I do and have no need for a file system!

- When I look through a catalog and see a gift idea, I rip it out and put it in the appropriate file. Even if I don't end up purchasing that exact item, it's nice to have ideas.

- The files are a great place to store directions to events such as weddings and parties. You can even keep tickets to future events in the appropriate month's file (instead of having them hang out on the fridge for four months).

I also have a selection of thank-you notes, thinking-of-you cards, and a few sympathy cards on hand for last-minute needs.

Step 5: Keep It Up

Set aside one day a week to do all your paperwork. If it's Wednesday, and this week Wednesday falls on the fourteenth, then all that week leading up to Wednesday, just drop any paperwork into the folder marked "14." I flag that folder with a giant sticky note so it's easy to drop papers into for review. Once I'm done with that Wednesday, I move the sticky note to the next Wednesday.

Keeping the STEM Strong

Space

So much for our paperless society, right? However, I do scan many items and file them on my computer. One piece of paper doesn't take up a lot of room, but when you multiply that by all the notes, reminders, mementos, and articles, we're talking binders' worth of paper.

Time

PUTTING IT BACK INTO PLAY

When it comes to paperwork, my biggest time-saver is something I call "Putting It Back into Play." When I get a piece of paper that requires an action (putting it on my calendar, paying it, returning it to a teacher, getting it back to church), my goal is to get that piece of paper "back into play" as quickly as possible by noting it on my calendar and then recycling the notice, writing the check, and sending the bill back in the same day's mail, or signing that permission slip and putting it in my daughter's backpack. The LOF is for anything that I can't deal with on the spot, so instead of letting the papers pile up on the kitchen counter, I place them in the file to deal with on a certain day. But if I can "Put It Back into Play" right away, then I've saved myself some additional steps. Big win!

I don't want that piece of paper fermenting in my house. Anytime a piece of paper sits around, it gets heavier. There are now fines to pay, excuses to make, and apologies to write. I want to get that ball into someone else's court, not to give them more work, but so they're no longer waiting on me to do their work.

Energy

Moving piles of paper takes energy. Don't let a piece of paper sit on your desk or counter; it invites friends. Get that paper back into play.

Money

Not being organized paper-wise comes with a financial cost. Late bills, last-minute trips to drop permission slips at school, lost checks, lost rebates, coupons that expire—they all total up to hundreds (if not thousands) of dollars lost each year.

Bonus Projects

1. Using the information from your home calendar, write on the inside of each hanging file the names and important dates of family events that occur annually. For instance, on the inside of the June hanging file in our house, I've written:

   12—Grandma Connie's birthday

   Father's Day

   14—Karen's birthday

   25—Our anniversary

   30—Kimberly's birthday

2. For one-time events (such as graduations and baptisms) write the information on a sticky note and place it on the inside of the hanging file along with the annual events.

Project 14

Travel

I travel a lot. I probably spend the night in a bed other than my own about fifty nights a year. Most of the time I'm in hotels, but I do hang out in the occasional guest room as well. Besides all the business and ministry travel I do, we spend a good portion of my husband's vacation days either visiting his family in Georgia, visiting my parents in Sacramento, in Lake Tahoe (our family's favorite close by vacation spot), or in a park named Disney.

My packing plan has to work for all those different scenarios. Yes, I take different clothes for each, but I find the biggest travel hassle is when I forget to bring my foundation or don't have the Advil I so desperately need after a long day of travel.

If you're waiting for my tips on how to pack for a flight so that you can get everything into one carry-on bag, you need to look somewhere else. I understand that luggage gets lost sometimes, but in the past six years of traveling more than the average bear, I've had my bags take a little side vacation only once. (They found their way back to me about ten hours later.) Airlines have improved their performance so much; I don't mind waiting around the extra ten minutes to grab my suitcase in baggage claim.

However, if you want to know how to have everything you need when you get there, I'm your girl.

Step 1: Your Plan of Attack

TOILETRIES

If you travel only once a year, you may want to gather these items up before your trip. If you're traveling more than a couple of times a year, I suggest you leave your travel toiletries packed and just refresh what you need before you leave.

CLOTHES

At least a week before your trip, make a list of the clothes you want to take (see my packing list at www.ProjectsForYourSoul.com). Remember, you may want more than one outfit a day (especially for dressier nights out or cruises), so be sure to list all of those as well.

Step 2: Sort It Out

As you're doing laundry the week before you travel, move all the clothes you plan to take on your trip to one space in your closet. I have a little section for this, so after my clothes are washed and dried, I hang them there so I won't be tempted to wear them and then have to stay up late the night before my trip doing emergency loads of laundry.

If you're packing for other people in your home, I suggest the same closet trick for them, but perhaps not in their closet. Also, I love having a tub or two in the laundry room for everyone's folded clothes and for shoes. The tubs take the clothes out of circulation, and it's easy to pack everything in one fell swoop.

Step 3: Label It

I have three separate bags for my health-and-beauty products: one for general bathroom items, one for makeup, and one for all the hair products I need to go from showered wet head to hopefully curly—not frizzy—redhead. (With the humidity in Atlanta, anything more Little Orphan Annie and less Ronald McDonald is acceptable.)

I use three separate bags because I always need to take the bathroom and makeup bag but not always the hair bag for an overnight trip. Sometimes I'll leave the bathroom bag in the hotel but take my makeup with me in my bag or car.

Here is what I keep in each:

Bathroom Bag

- Deodorant
- Feminine hygiene products
- Toothbrush (the kind with a built-in cover)
- Toothpaste
- Dental floss
- Hair spray and other hair products for touch-ups
- Comb
- Tweezers
- Nail file
- Nail glue
- Shower gel
- Lotion
- Fragrance
- Razor
- Extra razor blades
- Fashion tape
- Curling iron
- Teeny-tiny sewing kit

Makeup Bag

- Moisturizer
- Foundation
- Concealer
- Eyeliner
- Mascara
- Lid base
- Eye shadow (four pack)
- Blusher
- Lip pencil
- Lipstick
- Lip gloss

Hair Bag

- Hair dryer
- Shampoo and conditioner
- Diffuser
- Any other styling products

In addition to these bags, I have a tiny pouch where I keep a small supply of medications for such things as pain, indigestion, constipation, and anti-diarrhea. I can put this in my bag if I have a day trip and a headache.

Your Carry-On

While airline luggage handling has improved over the years, delays are still a frequent part of air travel. It seems like every time we have a connecting flight in Denver, we get to spend an additional two, three, or even ten hours enjoying their shops and restaurants.

With sometimes extreme lines for TSA screenings, my motto has become, "Come early, sit long, and relax."

Like a child that needs to be entertained, I need to pack my carry-on with enough toys and tricks to keep me amused for several hours.

Airports have finally gotten wise to the fact that we travel with our laptops and laptops require power. That's why no matter how short the trip, I bring a power cord. Here's a list of the other things I pack for a cross-country trip:

- Laptop/iPad with keypad and charger
- iPod
- Magazines
- A book
- Dried fruit or granola bar
- Travel mug (which I fill with coffee on the other side of security)
- Neck pillow and sleeping mask
- Small notebook
- Pen
- Sticky notes
- Shirt and underwear (packed in a Ziploc bag)
- Everything I normally carry in my purse

I know that seems like a ton, but once you've been stuck for six hours in LAX without your computer, you'll understand why I travel heavy.

Of course, if you're traveling with kids, this list will look very different. My friend Lynette travels to South Africa frequently with her husband and three kids. Between the special challenges of traveling with five people as well as traveling internationally, she has some special insight to offer:

> "When we travel to South Africa with our three young kids, I always make sure I'm ready for any circumstance. Traveling ten thousand miles and for thirty-six hours is miserable for anyone, let alone kids. To make sure that I don't stress too much, I've learned to be super organized. I make piles in my room for all five of us in at least the following categories: pajamas, swimwear (if appropriate), underwear (one for each day), and shoes. Then I try to think of any special occasions that will be happening while we're there and set out a whole outfit for each of us for that occasion. I won't make the same mistake I made with my husband when we went on our first cruise and he had to wear his tennis shoes with his suit to the formal dinner.

> "I always have pen and paper ready when I'm packing to write down anything I think of that still needs to be packed but is in the wash or I need to buy. I pack a small supply of toiletries for the plane so that we can be semi-fresh when we arrive in South Africa.

> "I pack minimally because I know that we can do laundry where we're staying. I don't like to take too much luggage when we travel, so I usually have a two-suitcase limit. This way, when we pick up our bags in baggage claim, it's not a huge problem.

> "The kids take their backpacks on the plane with them. They are responsible to pack a favorite soft toy, blanket, and book. I make sure to pick up some coloring supplies, snacks, and toys (that don't make loud noises) that I give to them on the plane as a surprise. These also come in handy at airports as we usually have lengthy layovers.

"Traveling with kids isn't easy, but I've learned that the more organized I am, the better the trip starts and the easier the journey is for all of us."

Step 4: Keep It Up

When I'm on a trip and realize that my shower gel or other item is less than half full, I make a note in my phone (I have a list program in there) to pick it up the next time I'm at Target.

Keeping the STEM Strong

Space

You want to make every item you pack do as much for you as you can. When we went on cruises before, I would pack four different formal/semiformal outfits, each requiring their own set of shoes and a bag. Now that I've gotten a bit older (and hopefully wiser), I realize that no one is going to notice if I have the same basic shoes and bag each night. I now take along a pair of cream strappy sandals with a gold sheen to them and a very light gold bag that's so cute my daughter borrows it for weddings. Your colors may be silver or black, but get something basic and let your clothes and your jewelry make the splash.

Time

While I don't want a neon-orange pom-pom tied to my suitcase so I can identify it, I do have a set of turquoise luggage tags that stand out and look cool. This saves time when it comes to scouting for my bag (and not picking up four black suitcases identical to mine). I also put one of my business cards with my cell phone number on the inside of the suitcase. If it goes missing and the tag is lost, at least my underwear is traceable.

Energy

A good old-fashioned shower cap will save you having to redo your entire hairdo when you shower.

Money

I keep a tiny funnel in my bathroom for refilling my travel-sized containers. You pay for the words "travel-sized" on any product you get (especially specialty shampoos and conditioners), but you pay pennies on the dollar when you refill from your larger products in your bathroom.

Bonus Projects

I've found pulling together a travel "comfort kit" for long airplane rides has been a lifesaver. My kit includes:

- Noise-canceling headphones
- Neck pillow
- Night mask (for red-eye flights)
- Lightweight poncho that can be used as a blanket

Also, if you want to watch any movies or TV shows on your computer, iPod, or iPad during your flight, don't try to download them the night before you leave. Figure it out a week in advance and then download them over the week. You don't want to stay up late because you were having technical difficulties downloading a season of *Project Runway*.

TIPS FOR TRAVELING WITH CHILDREN

"When my children were little and I sent them to stay with their grandparents for a week, I packed each outfit (top, shorts, socks, underwear) in a gallon Ziploc bag so no one had to worry about matching outfits. It helps clothes not to wrinkle, and once the clothes were dirty, they simply put them back into the bag. I practiced the Ziploc bag technique for years and still use it for my T-shirts when I go camping and can't iron wrinkled clothes. If you press out all the air before sealing the bag, it reduces the wrinkling and the bags just slide around in your suitcase."—Mer

Robin Neil, owner of Are We There Yet Travel, offers the following suggestions to help make traveling with children less stressful:

> To help build excitement for the trip, make a countdown paper chain, one link for each day until the trip, and hang it in your kids' room. Then every night before bed, tear off one link. As the days get closer, the excitement really builds.

> Purchase disposable items, such as disposable bibs, antibacterial wipes, even plastic eating utensils. When you're done with the items, just toss. When traveling out of the country with children, especially if one parent only may accompany the children, make sure that you have a signed and notarized letter from both parents stating that permission is given to the accompanying parent (or temporary guardian) to take the child out of the country. Make sure also that the accompanying parent or guardian also has the necessary medical release forms for those children.

> Discuss the security clearance process with your children so they won't be frightened or surprised. Don't travel with toys that could be mistaken for weapons. If you have photo IDs for your children, bring them.

> Bring snacks, snacks, and more snacks. Airline food (if available) is not always appealing to young children. Make sure you ask ahead of time for a children's meal. Always bring your own snacks. This is reassuring to children knowing they will have their own favorite things to munch on during a trip.

> Think light. Toys that have many uses are the best. Buy a package of pipe cleaners (my kids love the neon ones), which can be made into any shape and then made into something else. Other great activities have been *one* long book for the older set (think Harry Potter) to keep them busy for long periods, and white, unlined paper to be used for drawing, folding, etc.

> Take individually wrapped hand wipes. These are great for

faces, hands, and stains on clothing. You can also bring Shout Wipes, which work wonders as well.

Make a surprise bag for each child that they cannot open until they get on the plane or in the car. Some people wrap a new toy or present for every hour of the trip and put those in a bag. As each hour comes, the child gets to open a new toy. You can purchase them from the dollar store or, if you're like us, you can use the stash of toys in the garage that they haven't seen in a while.

Books on tape are always a hit. Felt books are a *big* hit in our house. They come in most every character and can be hours of fun. Colorforms are a great idea also.

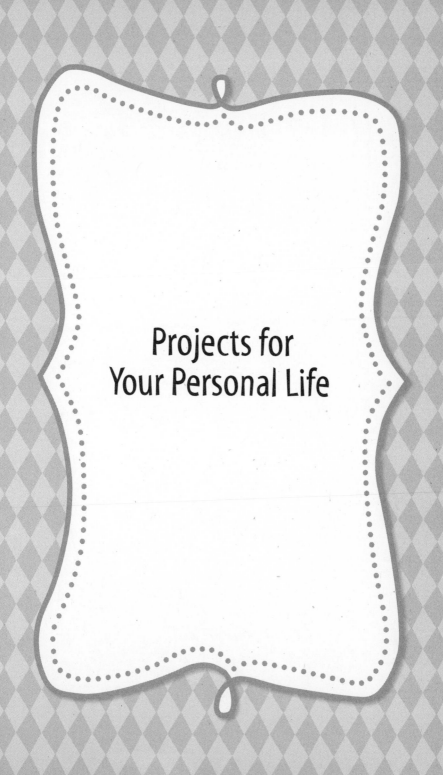

Projects for
Your Personal Life

Project 15

Your Schedule

I was talking recently with an acquaintance who was convinced she had a book that was going to change the world. She felt it was a literary masterpiece and was going to turn the publishing industry on its ear.

The problem was, she hadn't written it yet.

You see, she's a stay-at-home mom (although her kids are in school most days from 8:00 to 3:00, September through May), and she is *just so busy.*

- She volunteers as a room mom.
- She's involved with PTA.
- She's on the steering team of her MOMs group.
- All three of her kids are involved in sports.
- Two of her kids are involved in a theater group.
- Her entire family is involved in various church activities.

Therefore, the life-changing book is going to have to wait until she has more time.

I hear this almost any time someone asks me, "So, what do you do for a living?" Everyone wants to write a book, but nobody has the time.

I want to tell people who are convinced they must write a book (or do anything else they feel God is directing them to) that they are never going to see that happen unless they stop working for other people and start working for themselves.

You Determine Your Schedule

I'm always amazed at the women who feel hopeless when it comes to their schedules. Yes, maybe you work for a boss who determines much of your schedule, or maybe you have the overwhelming feeling that your kids run your schedule. Ultimately, however, you are the one—or need to become the one—who determines how you spend your time.

You are not a bad parent by not signing your kids up for every activity that the school, community center, or church offers. You need to realize that when your kids say yes, that means you say yes. And sometimes you need to just say no.

Agree in Advance on What You Say Yes To

My husband and I talk a lot about what we will say yes to when it comes to time spent outside of pursuing our goals. Want to take me to coffee to talk about marketing your book? Meet me at Starbucks. Need me to bring you a meal because you broke your ankle? Dinner is in the oven—or more likely the freezer (but I'll warm it up for you!). Want me to help you move? Dude, I'm forty plus years old. Be a grown-up and hire a mover or pay some high schoolers. (I used to spend my weekends going out, but because I've helped people move, now my back is the one that goes out on weekends.)

Make sure you have someone to hold you accountable so you don't say yes when what you really mean is, "I don't want to, but I don't want to hurt your feelings by telling you no." If you can say, "My husband (mom, friend, accountability partner, boss) and I agreed I wouldn't say yes to anything that wasn't (part of my job description, related to photography, discussed in advance)."

If you have a hard time saying no to people, an excellent book for you to read is *The Power of a Positive No* by William Ury.

Have One Calendar

In a previous chapter, we talked about how to manage your family's schedule. However, for me, nothing happens—not for me or my kids—unless it's on my calendar. I've trained my kids that if they want to make sure I show up someplace, they need to either email it to me or stand over me as I'm putting it on my calendar.

Yes, you will have a family master calendar, but every single appointment you need to show up for—every pickup and drop-off—everything—needs to be on your personal calendar.

Manage Your Energy, Not Your Time

Tony Schwartz is the president and CEO of the Energy Project, which helps people and organizations fuel engagement and productivity by drawing on the science of high performance. He is also a coauthor of *Be Excellent at Anything*.

After understanding more about his research, here are some of the ways I have changed my workday to be more clear-minded and focused:

- I work for ninety minutes at full capacity, and then take a break to recover.

- After spending concentrated energy on a task (writing, preparing a speech, anything math related), I switch to something that fills me up—taking Jake for a walk, having a conversation with a fellow author or speaker, brainstorming and dreaming about a project.

- At about 2:00 most days, I take a fifteen-minute nap.

This may seem like a series of indulgences. In fact, it's the smartest way I know how to work. "The reality is that if a person works continuously all through the day," Schwartz says, "she'll produce less than a person of equal talent who works very intensely for short periods and then recovers before working intensely again."

Working Outside the Home

Even those of us who work forty hours plus a week have many hours left over in our week. Even at work, most of us have some say in how and when our work gets done.

If you're dragging after a long day of work, is it only work that's wearing you out or are other habits leading to perpetual exhaustion? I know I get a poor return on investment if I stay up late trying to get things done. Instead, if I get up earlier in the morning, followed by going to bed at a decent hour, I will get almost twice as much done because I have more energy and my mind is sharper.

If you laughed at the sentence above about taking a nap at 2:00, don't be so quick to chuckle. Many high-level executives have started taking a pillow and blanket to work. As far back as I can remember, my mom, who worked as a social worker and data input coordinator for over thirty years, would close her office door or face away from her cubicle opening and "power nap" for just a few minutes. I used to think that people who napped just needed to suck it up and be big kids. Now I see the brilliance in their strategy.

I'm new to the whole napping thing, but I have to say I feel like I get two mornings every day. My naps aren't long (if I let them go over twenty minutes, I wake up a bit foggy), and I easily make up the time with clearer thinking and more energy.

Working Inside the Home

If you have small kids or are homeschooling, yes, you're contending with other people's schedules. However, something I realized late in life was that my kids' time was no more valuable than mine was.

It's OK if my kids have to wait an extra twenty minutes to be picked up from an activity or friend's house if I can combine trips with picking up another kid. (I'm thinking here of older kids who are perfectly OK hanging out without adult supervision.) Don't be afraid to say, "No, I won't go fifteen minutes out of my way to drop you off at home so you can watch TV. You can help me with the groceries, thank you very much."

Office Hours

If you stay at home, don't fall for the trap that you're available for everyone, all the time. I've had to establish my own office hours where

I just can't be disturbed. I start to write in the morning at about seven, and except for a brief chat with my son as he's on his way to work, I'm in lockdown mode. I don't answer the phone, I rarely check email, and I plow through until about nine.

That means I rarely meet people anymore for breakfast or coffee before noon. I can meet for lunch or an afternoon Starbucks, sure. However, my most productive hours are between seven and nine in the morning, so I save those for the activity that requires the most brainpower. (Yes, it's longer than ninety minutes, but in the morning I don't feel the need to lay my head down on my desk.)

Your schedule will look very different from anyone else's, and every day has a rhythm to it.

Keeping the STEM Strong

Space

When it comes to scheduling space, we all need to make sure there's a buffer in our calendars. Kids get sick, projects take longer than expected, and our bodies need rest. I actually have whole weeks where I write "BOOK NOTHING" on my calendar. That means no extra appointments, no extra work, no out-of-town events.

Time

Make sure you schedule time for your family as well. Dates with my kids—coffee at Starbucks before school, lunch at a salad bar, or just driving together with the iPod off—were important times for connecting.

Energy

We call it my Early Warning System. If I know I'm facing a rough deadline, I tell the people I know and love that it's going to be a stressful time for me. My mom, being the gracious woman she is, knows that if there's an emergency, of course I want to hear from her. But our catch-up talks on day-to-day life? She waits for me to pick up the phone.

My husband and I try to balance out the energy and stress in our lives. I know that Easter and Christmas are extra busy times for him because of events at church. I try to not book anything around these times so that I can keep the home fires burning (i.e., make sure we have food in the house, keep laundry going, and feed the herd regularly). He does the same for me while I'm traveling or near a book deadline.

Money

Remember the real cost of all your activities. If you volunteer twice a week at your kids' school, and those always happen to be the nights that you drive through the Golden Arches, don't ignore the situation. An overcrowded schedule can lead to a real financial strain on your family. Make sure you evaluate all the costs—dinners out, purchasing convenience food, gas, babysitting—of giving away your "free" time before saying yes to adding to an already packed schedule.

Bonus Projects

USE THE BUDDY SYSTEM

> "With four kids (all active) and a busy husband, I have to keep on top of things. Once a week I meet with a friend, and we intentionally plan for the week ahead. I take our home/family notebook, family and personal calendars, and meal planner, and get it done. We include a cleaning schedule, daily activities, and meal planning. I find it helpful to plan everything out all the way down to my personal time. But I also remember I can always make adjustments if needed."—Claudia

Project Reports

> "I like your idea of accountability. If you run opportunities and requests by your husband/friend/mom, it gives you a cooling-off period from the excitement of the request. Have you noticed so many leaders are great salespeople? They get

you excited about something, and before you know it, you're signed up to coordinate the giant potluck at the high school (not that I'm bitter or anything). *The Power of a Positive No* is a great book to read about how to say no gracefully and graciously."—Susy

Project 16

Getting Out the Door in the Morning

Getting out the door is all about the night before. Let's all say it together: "Getting out the door is all about the night before."

The following is a mental checklist I run through each night to make sure everything runs smoothly and on time for my family and me the next morning. If you have kids over the age of six, you should divide and rotate some of these duties among other family members so you're not the only one helping in a way that benefits everyone.

The Night Before

1. Check backpacks and make sure everything your child's teacher is expecting to show up is in there.

2. Pack lunches.

3. Set out clothes for you and your kids.

4. Place backpacks, purses, and briefcases by the front door.

5. Charge cell phones.

6. Make sure your gas tanks contain gas.

7. Move anything that needs defrosting for tomorrow night's dinner from the freezer to the fridge.

8. Set up coffeemaker with water and grounds.

9. Set out cereal bowls, dishes, and glasses for breakfast.

10. Set out your thermos and water bottles (or chill water bottles in the fridge).

11. Charge your laptop.

12. Set alarm clocks.

13. Place keys where you can find them.

14. Empty the dishwasher so the morning dishes can go directly into it.

15. Shut off your computer at least an hour before you plan to go to bed. Your brain needs some transition time.

16. Go to bed on time.

The Morning Of

1. Stagger bathroom times if you have multiple people using the same bathroom.

2. If you have a half bath in another part of the house, one child can use that for everything but the shower.

Keeping the STEM Strong

Space

"If someone has to use the half bath, all their stuff (toiletries, makeup, hair dryer) should be stored in there. If not, it will never be available in the right place at the right time. You may even want to buy a duplicate set of some items."—Rita

Time

"Our family discusses at dinner time anything that's different in the schedule for the next day—a child needs to be at school early, a parent has to be to work early, lunch is provided so there's no need to make a lunch, they're having special spirit days at school and your child can wear only orange and purple, and so on."—Jennifer

Energy

As my kids got older, I made sure they took on more and more of their lunch-packing chore. At first it was just picking out a fruit and a snack that they wanted to take. Eventually, the whole chore became their responsibility.

And as kids get older, they need to be more and more in charge of their morning routine. When my kids were in junior high and high school, I wanted to know that if I had to leave early for work or (gasp!) sleep in because I wasn't feeling well, they could handle all the "get up, get ready, get out" chores themselves.

Money

> "If there's something out of the ordinary you have to take with you (perhaps a movie to return or package to mail), go ahead and put it in the car. That way you can't forget it and you'll save a lot on late fees. I have stepped over many a thing placed by the front door where I 'couldn't miss' them."—Rita

Bonus Projects

GET YOUR SUNDAY MORNINGS IN ORDER

When my kids were in elementary school, we had a children's pastor, Jim Lyman, who made Sunday mornings the "can't miss" event of my kids' week. Between the puppets, the skits, and the games, my kids were learning more about the Bible in that ninety minutes every Sunday than they were from me and their private Christian school combined.

Justen and Kimberly never wanted to forget their Bibles, and they always wanted to be sitting front and center each service. Therefore, we had a bag that was just for Sunday mornings. It had an extra Bible in it, anything they were supposed to bring to church, and their "church bucks" that they earned for bringing their Bibles, bringing friends, and memorizing Scripture. That bag saved us a lot of stress on Sunday mornings.

> "I used to spend Sunday mornings running through the house turning out lights and throwing breakfast food back in the fridge while the rest of my family sat in the car with the engine running. ('Where is she? Why is she taking so long! Mom! I might be late to children's worship!') Now each family member is responsible for one 'leaving the house task' so we can get out the door more smoothly."—Robin

Project 17

Your To-Do List

Everyone has a To-Do List. I just want to make sure yours is on paper.

When women tell me they don't work off a list, I know it's not really true. The list may be their email in-box, their calendar, or in their head, but everyone has a list.

So why am I so insistent that you put it down on paper? Because your brain is too important and busy to be used to remember all that stuff.

If you have all your to-dos and need-tos written down in a safe place, then your brain can relax and enjoy life, be creative, and love others well. But when your brain is constantly worried that you're going to forget to bring a dozen store-bought cupcakes to the teacher appreciation day at school, your brain is going to worry about those cupcakes, stress about those cupcakes, and wake you up in the middle of the night because of those cupcakes.

So, right now, I want you to find everything that's weighing on your brain, everything that's hiding in your email box, and every piece of paper in your house that's waiting for attention and put those things on a To-Do List. Here are some different options for recording your To-Do Lists:

- *A piece of paper.* It may seem quaint and old-fashioned, but for some of us, this is the best option.
- *A notebook*

- *A Task Manager* on your computer (such as the one in Outlook)

However you do it, you're going to need two kinds of lists.

The Master List

This is that list for the things currently weighing on you and waking you up at night. All those things that you think to yourself, *I should get _____ done this week (or month)*, but they just keep spinning around in your mind. This is the list where you write down the sink that needs to be replaced, the article on growing a salsa garden at home that needs to be written for your friend's blog, and your best friend's baby shower that needs to be organized. Anything that you want to/ need to take action on in the next month should be written down on your Master List.

Under each of your Master List items, you'll need a list of *next steps*. These are the steps you'll need to follow to complete any project on your Master List. Some initial next steps, for example, on the projects I mentioned above might be: look online at homedepot.com to see what kind of sink you need, check out books at the library on growing tomatoes in small spaces, and call your best friend to compare calendars for available shower dates.

The To-Do List

This is the daily list you take with you everywhere. This list is filled with next steps but no Master List items unless they can be accomplished in under fifteen minutes. The Master List is to make sure you don't miss anything you need to accomplish; the list of next steps is to make sure you don't get overwhelmed. Your daily To-Do List is filled with next steps.

So at home, as I'm stressing about all that needs to be done, I grab my Master List and write those things down:

- Replace bathroom sink

- Write blog article
- Organize baby shower

Once I have those on my Master List, I begin to write down the next steps under each one:

Replace bathroom sink

1. Look up styles of sinks at homedepot.com

2. Find out what size sink we need

3. Call Sue to find out name of contractor

4. Meet with contractor

5. Order sink

Write blog article

1. Check out tomato books at library

2. Find out word count for article

3. Talk with Master Gardener at extension program about soil

Organize baby shower

1. Check with Angela re: available Saturdays

2. Check with Angela's mom re: dates

3. Pick up invitations

4. Ask Vikki and Michelle to help with party

If you know your Master List is going to contain some complicated items, you may want to dedicate a whole page to breaking it down into next steps.

So every day, as I pull together my To-Do List for the day, I look over the next steps and figure out a few things I can do that day that will get me closer to my goal.

People get overwhelmed by a To-Do List because they have a lot of Master List items on there—things that require a whole series of actions and aren't broken down into simple, doable steps. It's a great way to set yourself up for failure.

So today, gather everything that's weighing on you and figure out what list it belongs on. If the whole thing takes less than fifteen minutes, you can put it on your To-Do List. If it's more complicated than that, put it on your Master List and figure out what your next steps are.

Project Report

> "I have a cheap little notebook in the top drawer of my night-stand, and if I do wake up in the middle of the night with something nagging at me, I scribble it on the pad. Then I can easily go back to sleep knowing I can't forget it. When I have a To-Do that didn't get done, I put it on another day, and I'm not responsible for it in between the day it *was* on and the day it is now reassigned to. This has made a huge difference in my life. I can actually tear out the page at the end of the day and crumple it up, which I like. If I move something to another day more than a few times, it's either too large for a daily list (and should be broken down into next steps) or it's a signal that I really don't want to do it or don't know how. If that's the case, I try to look for another way to get it done, such as hire someone or do some research so it's not such a block."—Rita

Project 18

Your Car

My friend Carol says, "I think a car is actually a mobile storage unit, like an extra closet—a purse on wheels, if you will." I say amen to that. There are times of the year when I virtually live in my car. And yes, it is sometimes like a giant handbag, holding all my essentials (and nonessentials).

Sometimes it's my mobile house as well. It's my workstation and command post while I'm traveling (but not while I'm driving). It contains my entertainment system, my closet when I'm storing extra clothes for on the road, and sadly, sometimes my dining area.

When my kids were little, I occasionally would spend entire days in the car. And that's when problems can arise.

> "My car is the one that each time the door opens, some piece of garbage goes flying out. It drives me crazy. I feel like the Jed Clampett of car owners."—Jenny

Many of us can identify with Jenny. For some reason, cleaning out our car is the last thing we want to do. It seems like a chore we can always do later.

Step 1: Your Plan of Attack

Figure out where's the best place to clean your car. For most of us it's going to be in the garage or the driveway. However, I love my friend Gwen's idea and have been following suit:

"Sometimes I have to actually drive elsewhere to clean out my car, even if I don't have to go anywhere. Otherwise, it becomes the one job that can always happen later. I bring paper grocery bags with me and use one bag for trash, another bag for stuff that has to come into the house, and one for things to recycle. Even if I don't want to wash my car, sometimes I'll go to the car wash to clean out my car and throw junk away there. It's just a mental thing. I know it would be just as easy to do this in my driveway (probably easier), but sometimes I have to trick myself."—Gwen

Besides location, make sure that you make the chore as pleasant as possible. Blast some tunes on your stereo and promise yourself a drive-thru Starbucks as a reward for keeping your mobile home clean and shiny.

Step 2: Sort It Out

Here's another instance where you can use the three-box, two-bag system. Or if using bags rather than boxes is easier (and your car is small), that can work as well.

OTHER ROOMS

In this box or bag, put everything that you want to keep that doesn't belong in the car. The items in this box are the only ones from your cleanup that should make it back into your house.

PUT BACK

As you decide what to keep in your car, here are some items to consider. It may seem like a long list, but most of these could fit into a big shoebox and many can go in your glove box. Don't go out and buy everything at once, but start gathering your collection now and keep anything on this list in the car:

- *Owners' manual.* Make sure this is in your glove box. It has a lot of useful information, not just about your car but also basics like how to change a tire.

- *Maps.* GPS rocks—until it doesn't.

- *Blankets.* An absolutely essential item in cold weather, we have used these in the summer for nonemergency picnics.

- *Bottled water.* Great in an emergency, or when you're having to wait for your kids to finish in overtime and it's 101° outside.

- *Snacks.* I've never had to use these in an emergency (unless you consider a cranky two-year-old an emergency). These are things like prepackaged dried fruit, nuts, and jerky.

- *Jumper cables.* Whether you need help or can offer it to someone else, jumper cables are the Good Samaritan's best friend.

- *First-aid kit (and manual).* Everyone should have a basic kit, not just in case of an auto accident but so you can be the prepared mom when you're at the park or involved with other activities.

- *Towels.* Having a couple of old beach towels has saved us a few times when we needed to dry off a wet kid, protect my back seat after a muddy soccer game, and provide a place for Roger to lie on as he put on snow chains.

- *Tiny umbrella.* You'll bring your big umbrella in a downpour, but it's great to have a tiny one for those spring showers.

- *Garbage bags.* These have come in handy several times, whether it's cleaning out the car or providing weatherproofing in the snow and rain. (You have to be careful with plastic garbage bags around little kids, of course.)

- *Phone charger.*

- *Disposable camera.* In case you're in an accident and the camera feature on your phone isn't working.

- *Your insurance information.*

- *Fix-A-Flat tire sealant and inflator.* This little miracle-in-a-can is able to get you to the next gas station while not riding on your rims

- *Road flares.* I hope you never have to use these, but if your husband is lying on the side of the road changing a flat, you'll be glad to have them.

- *Flashlight.* We have a hand-crank flashlight, but if you're using a battery-operated one, make sure you have fresh batteries.

- *Fire extinguisher (five pound).* If you're in an accident (or even if you're not) and there's a small fire, a fire extinguisher can stop something that otherwise could turn into a disaster.

And here are some wintertime items you should consider having in your car:

- *Road salt.*
- *Shovel.*
- *Hat, scarf, and gloves.*
- *Old cellular phone.* This should be powered off with a fully-charged battery (you'll probably need to recharge it periodically). Most old cellular phones, even an inactive one, can be powered on to call 911 as long as it still has a SIM card.

- *Battery-powered radio.* Include extra batteries or have a hand-cranked radio.

- *Portable battery charger.* A few of the items on this list require batteries (I recommend rechargeable ones). A portable battery charger can plug into your car and recharge any batteries that are dead.

- *Change of clothes.* These have come in handy more than once for a child or for a husband who had to lie in the snow to put tire chains on. When the kids were little, I kept a full change of clothes in the car for each of them. Now I just have an extra sweatshirt for each of us just in case.

GIVE AWAY

You've been great about your Give Away boxes from cleaning out your house, saving up all your treasure for the next time you go to the drop-off location at your favorite charity. The problem is, there probably isn't a convenient time for you to drop off your stuff. Take a moment this week and take it all in. You'll feel like you've lost five pounds without hitting the gym.

GARBAGE AND RECYCLING

I love Stephanie's motivation for keeping her car clean:

> "I put trash in the pocket of the driver door that I empty at every gas fill-up, which these days is often, and every night the car is emptied to start fresh the next day. Incentive? I *have* to have a free cupholder for the day's coffee supply."—Stephanie

Step 3: Clean It Up

I keep a package of sanitizing wipes in my car, and this is when I use them the most. When I'm decluttering my car, I also go through it and wipe it down. I also love to declutter at the gas station or car wash where I can use one of the vacuums to clean the floors and upholstery.

Step 4: Label It and Put It Away

You know what will fit best for your car. Maybe it's a tote bag carrying all your extras or a file box that holds emergency supplies. Here is how my friend Cindy handles it in her tiny car.

> "In my passenger seat, I have an open carryall with a handle to store tissues, trash bag, sunscreen, a water bottle, pens, pencil, pad of paper, and ball cap. If someone needs to ride in the front seat, the whole carryall can be lifted into the back seat. All the 'normal' papers and trash tend to get stuffed into my purse because I don't want to clutter up my car!"—Cindy

Whatever system you use, make sure things are labeled so you'll find it natural to put things back where they belong.

Step 5: Keep It Up

Gas fill-up solution. Every time you fill up your car, clean out your car. The trash can is right there. This is my number one way of keeping my car looking less than trashy. And if you need some extra incentive to keep your car clean, try this *take-a-friend-to-lunch solution:*

> "Offer to pick up a friend for lunch or coffee. You can be sure you'll clean out your car first because you know that *no one* likes to ride in someone else's messy car."—Michele

When my kids were in junior high, I had a great way of keeping the car clean. My kiddos were notorious for calling "Shotgun" as soon as I announced we were going anywhere. I finally made a rule that whoever was riding up front with me was responsible for gathering up any trash, extra clothes, and other stuff that had accumulated and for putting those things away.

Keeping the STEM Strong

Space

> "I have a divided wire basket that fits between the front seats in our minivan. It holds activities for kids on one side and Mom's menagerie of junk in the other side. It's a beautiful thing!"—Amberly

Time

Put Your Kids to Work (but don't let them eat)

> "We clean out the car when we get out. If I see junk lying around on the floor, the kids and I don't get out until we pick it up. I do a lot of business in my car, and I keep my products in suitcases or containers I can easily remove. I also limit eating in the car to long trips. There is really no need to have

a car full of crumbs and food wrappers. I love a clean car!"—
Shawna Lee

Energy

If you have small kids who snack in your car, you may want to try
Robin's approach to car maintenance:

> "Have a dog? Put it to work! When my kids were little, I would
> bring Tiny the dachshund out to the car to eat all the Cheerios
> and Goldfish crackers off the seats and carpet. And he thought
> I was the hero for allowing him the privilege! I also believe that
> any kids old enough to not be in a car seat (and some who are)
> should be part of the cleanup crew. Plus, it's easier for little
> kids to get in the way back of my van to clean it out."

Money

Emergency money. I keep a small amount of cash in my car for toll
roads, tow-truck driver tips, and the emergency latte. That money has
saved me twice from getting a ticket on a random tollway. Also, I
include a little stash of quarters for parking meters. (Watch one episode
of *Parking Wars,* and you'll never be without quarters again.)

Bonus Projects

Recently, I was hanging out with my godkids, Matthew and Lau-
ren, and their mom, Kimberly. Matthew is at that decidedly junior-
high age and is on the cutting edge of all things cool. Kimberly was
telling me that Matthew had a new adjective for their six-year-young
Volvo: *tragic.* So imagine how completely tragic his godmother must
be for driving a car so old, he couldn't believe it's still running. My van
is a dozen years old, but it's the sexiest car on the planet. You see, it's
paid for, and because I keep putting off getting a new car in order to
continue saving money, I splurge once a year and get the whole thing
"going to put it up for sale" detailed.

Your Handbag

I have a giant purse. Huge! I figure the bigger the bag, the smaller my rear end looks. Plus, as much as I'm on the road, I need to carry a lot of stuff with me.

I remember one time telling Roger that I needed a purse with wheels to lug around all my belongings.

"That's called a suitcase," Roger said. "And you have a problem."

I will always have a giant purse, but I don't need to have the back-and-shoulder pain that go with an overstuffed bag. And even if my purse were big enough to carry everything I own, I'd still need to be able to find a specific item in the midst of that cavernous bag.

Which for years I couldn't do. I can't tell you how many times I needed to dump out the entire contents of my purse in order to find a receipt I was looking for or a business card to give to a new friend. Not very professional looking.

Our handbags need to be set up to be used. It is possible to carry what you need (even if you subscribe to the "less is more" motto of handbags) and look like you have it all together.

Maybe your main bag is a beautiful square-shaped Michael Kors or a blue-and-white-striped diaper bag. Maybe it's your laptop bag or a backpack for the college classes you're taking. No matter what the outside looks like, you need a couple of containers on the inside to keep your life in order.

Step 1: Your Plan of Attack

In order to have an organized bag, you're going to need to gather a few tools to help you keep your stuff together.

A WALLET THAT WORKS FOR YOU

I had to go through a series of cute but impractical wallets until I found one that really worked for me. Yes, I sometimes get seduced into dreaming about a tiny pansy-covered wallet, the kind that would let me say, "Look, I can just stick it in my back pocket!" Or a sleek flat wallet, one that's so flat I wouldn't be able to carry anything in it. But I always come back to the style that is eerily like my mom's: one that has a bunch of slots for gift and credit cards, cash, and so on. I like the long, thin kind that has a place for a checkbook because I still have to write a couple of checks a month. It also keeps my business receipts better organized. Find a wallet that has a place for everything you carry:

- Cash
- Receipts
- Checkbook
- Credit, debit, and gift cards

All my photos are on my phone, so I don't carry around those wallet-sized pics. But if they are important to you, you might be able to find a wallet you love that includes a plastic picture holder.

THREE STORAGE BAGS

I prefer clear zippered or resealable bags of different sizes, but use what you have to get started. I use a large bag for makeup, a midsize one for emergency items, and a small one for change.

Step 2: Sort It Out

Here's my super-speedy way of cleaning out my bag. I simply take my purse and dump it out into a plastic grocery bag. I sort the dump into Other Rooms, Put Back, and (in this case) Throw Away.

OTHER ROOMS

Anything I want to keep that doesn't belong in my purse gets put away. This is also when I go through receipts I've carefully placed in my wallet (or the ones I've quickly thrown into my purse) and random notes or other pieces of paper. If you're away from home while you're sorting, just put these items into another bag to put away when you get home. And when you get home, *put them away in the right spot.*

PUT BACK

If it belongs in your purse, go ahead and put it back into your purse. (We'll get it better organized during Step 4.)

GARBAGE AND RECYCLING

Anything that's left over in your plastic grocery bag (food wrappers, cash receipts you don't care about, and so on) is now garbage that gets recycled or thrown away.

The beauty of the grocery-bag organizing system is that you can do it anywhere, anytime. Just grab a grocery bag and start sorting while you're waiting for your kids to get out of band practice or while you're on the phone with your mom.

Step 3: Clean It Up

Give your purse a good shake and get out any stray bits, crumbs, and the like. I've even used a handheld vacuum to really get the bag clean.

Step 4: Label It and Put It Away

Assign a spot for everything that belongs in your purse, bag, or backpack. This is where you use those three zippered pouches I mentioned a moment ago. Everything goes into one of those three pouches, into your wallet, or in rare cases (such as your sunglasses case, cell phone, and keys) simply into your purse or onto your key chain. The fewer items you place in your purse, the easier it is to know what's in there.

Wallet. I recommend you keep in your wallet only cash, receipts, checkbook, and credit, debit, and gift cards.

Pouch 1: Makeup bag

- Lipstick and gloss
- Eyeliner
- Powder
- Sunscreen stick

- Blush and brush
- Eyeglass cleaner wipes
- Hand sanitizer

Pouch 2: Emergency kit

- Fashion tape
- $20
- Needle and thread
- Nail glue

- Advil
- Couple of adhesive bandages

Pouch 3: Change

Step 5: Keep It Up

If I sort through the items in my purse once a week, it really is easy to stay on top of it. It takes only a couple of minutes to keep it up.

Keeping the STEM Strong

Once you've gotten into the habit of cleaning out your purse regularly, here are some extra steps to build your habit of creating a strong STEM.

Space

Now is a great time to sort through all those purses, backpacks, beach bags, computer cases, and briefcases you don't use anymore and give them to someone who would love them.

Time

Some of the biggest time-wasters are searching for your handbag and for your keys. Here are a couple of ways to help save you time.

Have a place for your bag, and put your bag in its place. For my mom, the place for her handbag was the hall-closet doorknob. For me, it's my shelf in my bedroom. Wherever it is, make sure everyone you live with knows exactly where your handbag goes so that when you need your kids to retrieve your cell phone, they know where to find it.

How to never lose your keys again (or at least 93 percent of the time):

> "I was forever losing my keys—in the house, in my jacket, in my purse, in the car, anywhere. I decided the madness had to stop, so I went to Walmart's key-making department and explained my dilemma. The salesclerk asked me to follow him down the camping aisle. We came to a display of hooky looking things, which he told me were carabiner clips. He asked for my keys, then attached one of the clips to my key ring and clipped the whole mess to the strap of my purse. Now I can hook the keys onto my purse, a tote bag, a backpack, a belt loop, even my fanny pack that I carry on my walks. Even my kids have learned to work the system so whenever they want the keys, they know where to find them. But more importantly they know where to *return* them."—Angela

Angela uses a carabiner clip. I use something similar designed for employees to clip their ID cards onto their waistbands. I clip mine to a zipper pull on the inside of my purse.

Energy

The mental-energy drain that comes with not having the right stuff in your purse is exhausting. If your medical insurance cards, your car insurance cards, or your credit or debit cards have expired, that can cause a lot of stress. Spend some time right now double-checking that everything you need (or might need) is up-to-date.

I thought I was updated until I tried to get onto a military base with an insurance card that had expired two days before. Here's a little piece of advice: don't try to enter a military base with anything out-of-date.

As I indicated earlier, I also carry a small bag of change with me. Not everyone will need this, but if you live in a place where you have to feed the meter, having change on you eliminates one more energy drain. You could also leave the change bag in your car as long as you don't have teens or young adults who think of it as the dollar-menu fund.

Money

Having a well-organized purse can actually save you money.

Food. I travel about ten weeks out of the year. All those breakfasts, lunches, and dinners add up. Some of those expenses can't be avoided, but if I have a couple of Starbucks VIA packets in my purse, I can have a great cup of coffee on the cheap. This happens mostly in hotel rooms where the coffee is often bad but the hot water is free. I put those little VIA packets in my emergency kit (because what's more of an emergency than the need for good coffee).

Gift cards. Did you know that about 10 percent of gift card dollars are never used? It's now considered a profit center by most major retailers. Don't let those dollars go unused! Whether it is twenty dollars left over on a Best Buy card or an unknown amount on a Target card you found at the bottom of your handbag, spend a little time investigating your assets. I go through my cards and check out the company website to find out my balance. Then in permanent marker, I write the total balance on the back of the card so I know how much I have to spend the next time I'm in the store.

Project Report

"Now that I've gone through this purse project, I'm hopeful that my purse will look less like a landfill, My friends always have some adorable bags that look so stylish, and mine always has all of these papers sticking out the top like some errant recycling bin. I love the idea of dumping everything into a bag and pulling out what you're keeping instead of the other way around. I'm always left with a pile of wads of gum in wrappers, wadded tissues, broken pencil points, and who knows what else that's tricky to grab out of my purse and get in the trash. Between old receipts and gift cards, my wallet usually resembles a pregnant pygmy goat. Now, after the clean out, I'm going to use a gift card or two this week!"—Robin

Project 20

Your Computer

How crammed is your email inbox?

When it comes to this time-saving technology, for me it can be as overwhelming as a messy room.

I receive between forty and a hundred emails a day in my main mailbox. Those are emails that, for the most part, I need to respond to. It can get a tad overwhelming. However, this week I got my inbox down to zero! Woohoo and neener-neener. (Yes, I am working on my Christlike attitude, thank you very much.)

Oh, and a little piece of advice—never tweet or post on Facebook that you've cleaned out your email inbox. Obnoxious friends you haven't heard from in months will send you email just so your inbox won't be empty anymore.

Staying on top of your email is critical. It frees you to let your brain think of other things because it's not spinning on all those people who are waiting by their computer for you to respond.

As much as email can be overwhelming, so too can all the files, folders, and just junk that sit on our hard drives and clutter our computer's desktop. Here are some ideas to keep your machine clean and organized.

Step 1: Your Plan of Attack

I'm going to assume that you have a basic knowledge of the files and folders on your computer. If not, you can google "Files and Folders for" and the name of your operating system to get some basic knowledge. Here's the best way I can describe them:

A file is a single item. Think of it as a single piece of paper, a bunch of pieces of paper that equal one document (like a contract), an article, a photo, a CD, a DVD, etc.

A folder is similar to an actual physical folder where you can put a piece of paper, a CD, and a photo all in the same place so they're easy to find. A folder is great for projects, all your photos from your snow trip, or the first chapter of your Great American Novel.

Step 2: Sort It Out

When my computer desktop is overcrowded, I set up three folders to sort everything out:

- Things to file
- Things to deal with right away
- Things to ask Roger about

Yes, I understand you may not have a Roger. (If I could clone him, I would be a very wealthy woman.) If you're not a computer engineer, perhaps you have one around you can ask (or at least you can ask your fourteen-year-old niece). I have very few things in my "Ask Roger" folder, but I want a measure of security before I start deleting files willy-nilly.

OTHER ROOMS

> "Photos need to be sorted well and often because they are today's clutter trap, I believe. Pick a method and stick to it. Organize your photos into folders labeled by date, event, or group type (i.e., Disney Trip 2011). Go through photos every two to three months to make sure they're still worth saving. Clear any downloads and trash often. For *all* items, if you don't use it two or three times a week, it doesn't need to be on your desktop!"—Beth

GARBAGE AND RECYCLING

The best way to find things quickly is to dump the stuff you no longer need. Go through your folders and files often and delete those things you don't need. One way I do this is to open a folder and sort the contents by oldest to most recent. When I see a file that hasn't been touched in over a year, I can often delete it without even opening it.

Step 3: Clean It Up

Do your best to keep your computer desktop clean and clear. File things that need to be filed, and limit yourself to five to ten items on your desktop. When you have forty "important" files or folders on your desktop, you can't find what is truly important.

Step 4: Label It and Put It Away

Roger, a computer guy, has laid out a few rules for keeping our computer under control.

ORGANIZE FILES AND FOLDERS

There are really just a few principles for organizing the files and folders on your computer. Here are some general guidelines that you might find helpful:

1. *Be selfish.* OK, that's probably not a good recommendation for a Christian book on getting organized. But however you go about organizing your files and folders, it has to work for you. Many great systems are probably out there that don't work for the way you think. That's OK. Make sure that whatever system you choose works for you.

2. *Be obvious.* Ask yourself two questions:

   - If I were looking for this file today, where is the first place I would look?
   - A year from now, will I be able to find this file?

3. *Be consistent.* I'm not sure if this is more about consistence or persistence. Perhaps I should have said, "Be per-consistent." The point is that because of the sheer volume of files that we deal with, this stuff piles up and continues to

pile up. Having a consistent method of organizing your files—and being persistent enough to stick with organizing those files—pays off.

4. *Be lean and mean.* I don't know if you really need to be mean. Being lean in your organizational structure will help you put files in the obvious place. Too much structure and our files can get lost. Pick the top ten activities you use your computer for and create folders for those activities. Don't be afraid to put some subfolders inside those main folders. Just don't get carried away.

When All Else Fails, Search

I won't stoop to quoting Matthew 7:7 here (though I thought about it). Let's face it—we spend a lot of time with our computers. We have many files on our computers. At some point, probably more often than you'd like, you're going to need to find one of those files. You should spend a bit of time learning how to use your computer's "search" feature. It can do some amazing things.

For example, you can search for a document that contains the word *pepperoni*. (Now where did I put my world-famous pizza-fondue recipe?) You can search for files that haven't been modified for three years. That could be helpful if you ever want to clean out some old files. Just be sure to clean out only documents; arbitrarily removing old files could cause you to delete program files that will likely destroy your computer.

Check out your operating system's website to find out how to use your computer's search features. Here's a super-quick summary for how to do a search using a couple of common operating systems:

> *For Windows 7:* Click the round Windows icon (also called the Start button) in the lower left corner, then start typing.

> *For Mac OS X:* Click on the little magnifying glass in the upper right corner, then start typing and press return.

Your computer's search feature has a lot more to offer than just this. Check it out! It will save you a lot of time and headaches down the road.

Step 5: Keep It Up

Cheat when it comes to answering your email. If you receive a lot of the same kind of email, you may want to compose a form letter for your response. When people ask me how to become a speaker or author, I have a standard email I send—not because I don't care about the person, but because if I gave a personal answer to each and every one, I would never respond to anyone.

Keeping the STEM Strong

Space

One of the best ways I've found to keep my computer desktop uncluttered is to use one of my favorite pictures as the default background. If I have a picture of my family or of my cat, Zorro, for my desktop background, I don't want to obscure their faces with an unused folder. This little trick helps keep my desktop tidy.

Time

Just because someone sends you an email doesn't mean you need to read it. When I subscribe to an e-newsletter or an email group, I don't use my main email address. I have a free Yahoo email account for all those things I'm interested in reading, but if the week is busy, I don't feel bad if I just delete the whole list. None of them is waiting for a personal response from me. This saves me time in sorting through my own email box for things I have to respond to.

Energy

Every day I take a break from the Internet in order to focus on the things that need to get done work-wise. Yes, I am tempted to check my email, but if I do, I'm letting someone else decide the direction of my day.

Money

I put little reminders on my Outlook calendar of anything I've downloaded or purchased online that has an expiration date. That way coupons (and Groupons) don't go unused, things I've ordered from Amazon don't get forgotten, and I can match my orders with our credit-card statements.

Project 21

Your Wardrobe

Oh, the stress of getting dressed. It's one of the hardest things to do each day.

I remember my friend Robin writing down on a calendar each day what she wore to school or church, and I so wanted to aspire to be as organized as that. Now if five out of seven days a week I put together an outfit that is clean and matches, I feel like a runway model.

Step 1: Your Plan of Attack

I suggest that you divide this project into two sections—drawers and closets. Tackling one section at a time will keep you from getting overwhelmed. If you have closets and closets of clothes, then you'll want to take it one closet at a time.

These projects actually make me happy. I can clean out a drawer while watching something stupid on TV, and the work I'm doing keeps me from losing too many IQ points.

Step 2: Sort It Out

Take it one shelf, one clothes rod, or one drawer at a time. If I'm starting on the closet, I pull about twenty pieces of clothing out at a time. That's a reasonable amount to sort out in about fifteen minutes.

I can usually get a drawer organized in less than fifteen minutes. Plan on two drawers for every episode of TV you're watching.

OTHER ROOMS

Put anything in this box that you want to keep but doesn't currently

207

belong in your closet. If you have a weatherproof jacket and it's June, figure out in advance where your out-of-season clothing goes. Roger and I made a deal—when the third kid moved out, he got her room as an office and I got the hanging closet space. That's where my out-of-season clothes hang.

PUT BACK

This box is for all the stuff you want to keep in your closet or drawers. Hold on! We'll get to it really soon. If you have things in this section that are easily wrinkled, see if you can hang those things in another closet for now. I would hate myself if I caused any of you to have to re-iron something.

You may want to start a separate section for clothes that you love but they need a little attention before you can wear them again. I've learned my lesson, and I don't let un-ironed clothes hang in my closet. This pile includes things like those pants that have a missing button or that shirt where the stain didn't come out. (For the latter, but sure to try Lucinda's surefire stain-removal strategy from Project 8.)

GIVE AWAY

If your closet is overstuffed, I hope this is your biggest sort pile. Organizing expert Peter Walsh says that we generally wear 20 percent of our clothes 80 percent of the time. Wouldn't it be great if when you went to your closet, it was like picking chocolates from a Godiva box? You love everything in there, but you choose depending on your mood.

If you have lots of clothes that just need to be given away, you may want to consider a big black garbage bag instead of the usual "Give Away" box. When the bag is filled up, get it out of sight (preferably to your car). Once an article of clothing is in the big black bag, you won't be tempted to fish it out "just in case it comes back into style." *No!* Hands off. Just think how thrilled someone else will be to get your cute shirt, and then think of how often you'd be shoving it aside to get to the jeans you want to wear.

Garbage and Recycling

I can't imagine what you would put in the garbage except for random nonclothes items, but if a piece of clothing has more holes than a box full of Cheerios, it's time it hit the recycle bin. Yes, I know it's comfortable, but show a little self-respect. It's possible to be comfortable and cute at the same time.

Step 3: Clean It Up

Turn over empty drawers into a garbage bag, and then wipe them down and put them back into your dresser. Dust the shelves in your closet and vacuum or sweep the floor.

Step 4: Label It and Put It Away

Drawers

I think that every drawer should have a specific purpose. In my dresser, I have a drawer each for:

- Socks
- Underwear
- Pajamas
- Shirts
- Sweats

It doesn't matter who's doing the laundry in my house; it's easy to tell where my clothes go. Yes, I'm usually the one putting laundry away, but sometimes it's my husband or my daughter. My son would rather die than put away my unmentionables. It's mortifying enough that he has to run them through the laundry.

In my sock and underwear drawers, I use shoeboxes (sans lids) to divide these into the following categories. I like having them divvied up so I can see if I'm running short on underwear and need to do an emergency load (it happens):

Socks
- Short socks (to wear with athletic shoes)

- Long socks (to wear with pants)
- Tights, Peds, or anything else that's not a typical sock

Underwear

- Bras (sports and otherwise)
- Briefs
- Spanx and any other torture devices worn only when leaving the house

CLOSET

In my closet, I have those white plastic dividers that retail stores use to separate sizes on a rack. I got blank ones off Amazon and use a permanent marker to write the different categories that I want in my closet:

- Jackets
- Sweatshirts
- Long-sleeved shirts
- Short-sleeved shirts
- Tanks

- Dress pants
- Crop pants
- Jeans
- Skirts
- Dresses

SHOES

It's hard for me to determine what will work best for shoes in your space. I have a tiny closet with just a whisper of shelf space, and since I have an upper rack and lower rack in my closet, I don't want to obscure my shoes by hiding them amongst my jeans.

So I have a pocket shoe holder on the back of our bedroom door. Yes, I wish there were a better way, but for the moment, this is what works for me. Someday I'll have a walk-in closet. Until then, I keep my shoes where I can see them.

I save my limited shelf space for boots and clunky-heeled wedges. I know that most of these not-for-real-people organizing magazines would have you put all your shoes in clear lidded boxes. That's fine for your one pair of Carrie Bradshaw-inspired Manolo Blahniks, but your everyday flip-flops need to be readily accessible and easy to put away after you kick them off at night.

Remember Rule 5: "Treat Your Home like a Grown-Up Kindergarten Room." Label everything so you know beyond a shadow of a doubt where to put everything.

Step 5: Keep It Up

Make a few simple rules for yourself when it comes to your wardrobe:

1. Don't hang it up if it needs to be repaired, ironed, or cleaned. Clothes in your closet are only "ready to be worn."

2. Items are either hung up or put in the laundry or repair pile—not sitting around your room waiting to be taken care of later.

3. Don't hang on to anything that you don't love to wear, doesn't fit (unless you're currently attending Weight Watchers meetings), and doesn't make you feel fab.

Keeping the STEM Strong

Space

"Living in campus housing, we have tiny closets...a major switch from walk-in closets the size of small bedrooms. I love skirts and have a ton, but hanging them individually on skirt hangers was hogging up *all* of my closet space. I finally tried a multi-skirt hanger and loved it enough to buy seven of them (yes, I have that many skirts). Then I did the same with my pants/slacks."—Cheri

Time

"With three boys, we use the dot system. Our oldest gets one permanent marker dot on the tag of each of his clothes, middle gets two dots, and third gets three dots. When something is passed down, it's so easy just to add a little dot, and I don't have to try to remember what belongs to whom."—Jessica

Energy

"A major part of my bathroom clutter was my lack of jewelry organization. Either I kept everything knotted and lumped in a big ugly jewelry box or my jewelry was in different locations, especially cluttering my one drawer in the bathroom. I don't have counter space for a jewelry stand, so when I saw a wall-mounted jewelry organizer on Amazon, I snagged it. It has made a huge dent in cleaning up my bathroom chaos. Not only do I wear coordinating jewelry more often now because I can actually find things I want to wear, but it's pretty to look at too. I find that I can keep up with organization if there's a designated home that has room for the item I need to put back."—Wendy

"I am an organizer when I work with clients. The most common thing we do is organize clothes by style and by color—all tank tops by color, all short sleeves by color, all long sleeves by color. Dresses are by season and color and so on. Also, changing to all the same color or style of hanger makes a huge difference in the appearance of your closet."—Michelle

"Clean shirts get hung up on the right, and I wear the ones on the left. It makes a smaller wardrobe look more diverse since I'm not wearing the favorite shirt every week. I don't fold socks—we only needed that in the seventies when we all wore the colored striped socks."—Kevin

"I don't fold socks. Each person has the same type and color of socks, so they can just grab two out of the drawer. Also, I don't sort my laundry to wash it. I do if there's something new, but most stuff has been washed enough that it's not going to bleed, so it all just gets dumped in together. I then do laundry by room so I don't have to sort it out again when it's clean."—Jessica

"After I wash my work uniforms, I hang them in my closet in order, Monday through Friday. That way I don't have to think about what to put on at 5:30 in the morning."—Amberlyn

When we had three boys (my husband, my son, and my stepson) all living at home, they always battled over which Hanes socks were whose. ("No, mine have the gray lettering, not the black!") Finally we just got three different kinds of socks: Hanes, Nike, and no-name. Guess which guy got the no-name. Poor Roger.

Money

If all your boys are a bit more conducive to sharing, you could go Vicky's route:

"Since I had all boys, I bought all the same kind of socks. No more worries trying to match or sort. It's such a little thing, but it made doing laundry so much easier."

Wrap-Up

Congratulations! I'm proud of you not only for purchasing the book, but for actually putting some time, effort, and steps into getting your home (and life) in order. I'm sure by now you've seen many of the benefits that other women have seen by working through the projects:

- Thinking about the five-step plan every time you encounter a mess in your home
- Realizing that each task can be broken down into doable steps
- Finding items that you thought had been lost forever
- Enjoying a little more space and a lot more peace

I don't want this to be the end for you. My prayer is that you'll keep up on the steps long after you've finished the book. I want these routines to become a part of your everyday life so that you never feel buried again.

Here are a few ideas to keep you focused long after *The Get Yourself Organized Project* is over:

- *Keep up the accountability.* Ask your accountability partners if they want to continue to check in once a week to make sure you keep up on those problem areas of your house (kitchen counters, anyone?).
- *Establish a "Get Yourself Organized" day once a week.* On

Mondays, I sit down with all my paperwork and calendar and get my week in order. Have one day where you look at everything that's going on in your life and schedule in some time to keep up on those areas that can rapidly grow out of control.

- *Commit to doing* The Get Yourself Organized Project *at least once a year.* Make sure you get your money's worth out of this book. Use it over and over again to refocus yourself once a year to concentrate on your home and life. (Twice a year would be even better.)

Dear Reader,

Thanks for being a part of *The Get Yourself Organized Project*. One of the greatest privileges I have is to hear back from the people who have used my books. I would love to stay in touch.

E-mail: Kathi@ProjectsForYourSoul.com
Facebook: facebook.com/kathilipp.author
Twitter: twitter.com/kathilipp

Mail: Kathi Lipp
        171 Branham Lane
        Suite 10-122
        San Jose, CA 95136

Opportunities for input and discussion with other readers are available at www.ProjectsForYourSoul.com.

In His Grace,

Kathi Lipp

The Husband Project
21 Days of Loving Your Man—on Purpose and with a Plan

Keeping a marriage healthy is all about the details—the daily actions and interactions in which husbands and wives lift each other up and offer support, encouragement, and love. In *The Husband Project* women will discover fun and creative ways to bring back that lovin' feeling and remind their husbands—and themselves—why they married in the first place.

Using the sense of humor that draws thousands of women a year to hear her speak, Kathi Lipp shows wives through simple daily action plans how they can bring the fun back into their relationship even amidst their busy schedules.

The Husband Project is an indispensable resource for the wife who desires to

- discover the unique plan God has for her marriage and her role as a wife
- create a plan to love her husband "on purpose"
- support and encourage other wives who want to make their marriage a priority
- experience release from the guilt of "not being enough"

The Husband Project is for every woman who desires to bring more joy into her marriage but just needs a little help setting a plan into action.

The Marriage Project
21 Days to More Love and Laughter

More love, more laughter—more lingerie.

What would marriages look like if for 21 days, husbands and wives put their marriage on *project status*? Plenty of books describe how to improve marriage, how to save a marriage, and how to ramp up the intimacy in a marriage. In *The Marriage Project*, Kathi Lipp shows readers how to put the *fun* back in marriage with 21 simple yet effective projects, such as doing something they enjoyed together before they got married or flirting with their spouse via email or text messages.

Each of the projects contains:

- a project description
- suggestions for how to complete the project
- reports from other couples on how they accomplished the project
- a prayer
- a place to record project results

In addition to the daily projects, three bonus projects encourage couples to turn up the heat in the bedroom.

For couples who haven't given up on the dream of being head-over-heels with their spouse again, *The Marriage Project* provides just the right boost.

Included are tips on how to use *The Marriage Project* to revitalize marriages in a local church or small group.

The Me Project
21 Days to Living the Life You've Always Wanted

Most women in the midst of careers, marriage, raising children, and caring for parents set their personal goals aside. *The Me Project* provides women with fun and creative ways to bring back the sense of purpose and vitality that comes with living out the plans and dreams God has planted in their hearts. Kathi Lipp's warm tone and laugh-out-loud humor will motivate women to take daily steps toward bringing purpose back into their lives and give them the confidence they can do it in spite of busy schedules.

A woman who reads and applies *The Me Project* will

- discover the unique plan God has for her life and her role as a wife, mother, worker, or volunteer
- gather a community of like-minded women who want to make their goals a priority
- change her attitudes toward her roles in life, as well as how she approaches her personal goals

This handy guide coaches women to do one simple thing toward achieving their goals each day for three weeks, bringing a sense of vitality and exhilaration back into their lives.

The "What's for Dinner?" Solution
Quick, Easy, and Affordable Meals Your Family Will Love

For many women, dread turns to panic around 4:00 in the afternoon. That's when they have to answer that age-old question, "What's for dinner?" Many resort to another supermarket rotisserie chicken or—worse yet—ordering dinner through a drive-thru intercom.

The "What's for Dinner?" Solution provides a full-kitchen approach for getting dinner on the table every night. After putting Kathi's 21-day plan into action, women will

- save time—with bulk shopping and cooking
- save money—no more last-minute phone calls to the delivery pizza place
- save their sanity—forget the last-minute scramble every night and know what they're having for dinner

The book includes real recipes from real women, a quick guide to planning meals for a month, the best shopping strategies for saving time and money, and tips on the best ways to use a slow cooker, freezer, and pantry.

With Kathi's book in hand, there's no more need to hit the panic button.

To learn more about other Harvest House books
or to read sample chapters, log on to our website:
www.harvesthousepublishers.com

HARVEST HOUSE PUBLISHERS
EUGENE, OREGON